The Ewes Valley

Book already published by the author:
The Railway to Langholm (ISBN 0 9517858 0 X)

Book in preparation:
Memorials of Langholm Parish:
Staplegordon and Wauchope Cemeteries

The Ewes Valley

AN HISTORICAL MISCELLANY

Brenda I. Morrison

R. Bruce McCartney

First published in 2000 in the UK by

R. B. McCartney
"Cairndhu", Walter Street
Langholm
Dumfriesshire DG13 0AX

info@cairndhu.net
www.cairndhu.net

ISBN 0 9517858 1 8

Printed and bound by Meigle Printers, Galashiels

Contents

Foreword

THE generations come and go, and with the passing of each a little bit of our history ebbs away too. This book will help to stem the flow. Reproducing John Elliot's "Ewes Valley" will bring it to a new and wider audience and be of benefit to future generations. The authors' research and meticulous recording of the Kirk records and headstones in Ewes will be of great help to students of local history and genealogy.

Over the years, many families have come to the Parish, some stayed, many are spread throughout the land, others moved to far-flung corners of the world, but to any who are drawn back in body or imagination to the watergate of Ewes, the following pages will be of interest and a guide to all, old or young, at home or abroad.

DOUGLAS ELLIOT
Burnfoot of Ewes
6 April 2000

MEMORIAL 61

*Here lye JOHN ARMSTRONG of Sorbie who died March 17th 1685
aged 53 MARGARET MURRAY his spouse who died May 17th 1716
aged 76 years And JOHN ARMSTRONG their son who died November
6th 1698 aged 14 years "Whither thou be old or young think upon the
time to come"*

Introduction

Bотн of us have been delving into our respective family trees, at times pooling our ignorance, as well as our resources. When in contact with other researchers, we have heard, time and again, these requests from other folk: where do we go locally in Langholm? And what is available?

One place certainly to visit is Langholm Library in the Town Hall Building.

Langholm Library Trust extended ready access to us to use their reference books. We have been given permission to reproduced the main reference we used, "Memorials of Ewes Parish", compiled and indexed by the late George Gilchrist, F.S.A.(Scot.) from a survey by the late Robert A. Shannon, F.S.A.(Scot.) who also researched the Pardoned List. The booklet was produced as a typed document in 1968, with, in the main, only pre-1855 inscriptions.

We have taken the opportunity to make minor corrections and update the memorial inscriptions for Ewes and Unthank to 1950.

Langholm Library has also the Session Records of Ewes Kirk from 1717 to 1743 and from 1806 to 1905. In it, one of us found that an ancestor was refused a Testimonial from the Minister! There is also the intriguing Session Minute entry one month, "W. Young instructed to sell the bason." Followed in the next month, "W. Young reported that he had sold the bason."

We met requests from present day researchers asking about the Ewes Valley in which their ancestors lived: Hawick Archaeological Society readily gave permission for the late John Elliot's lecture, "Ewes Valley" to be reproduced. This lecture appeared in the Society's "Transactions" in 1953. We are sure that John Elliot's notes give an excellent insight to the Ewes Valley in the past. Minor changes have been made to the text to bring it more up to date.

The list of Ministers, the Centenary Leaflet, the Notes on Memorials and the Extracts will give readers an insight into Ewes Parish and its inhabitants.

We hope that *The Ewes Valley* will help both family historians and those interested in local studies: it could not have come about without assistance from several individuals: Alex. McCracken, B.Sc., F.S.A.(Scot.); Rev. Bob Milne allowed access to Ewes Kirk to record the information therein; Anne Elliot of Ewes Valley for her assistance, and to her husband, Douglas who wrote the Foreword; Graham Lumsden of Waverley Typesetters, Galashiels, gave invaluable help in the preparation of this book. To these individuals and to many others, we express our thanks.

In preparation are memorial inscriptions for the cemeteries in Langholm Parish.

BRENDA I. MORRISON
R. BRUCE McCARTNEY
Langholm
May, 2000

Ewes Valley

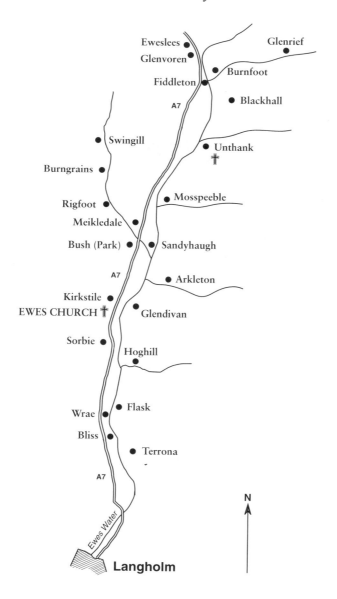

Eweslees

Glenrief

Glenvoren

Burnfoot

Fiddleton

A7

Blackhall

Swingill

Unthank

Burngrains

Rigfoot

Mosspeeble

Meikledale

Bush (Park)

Sandyhaugh

A7

Arkleton

Kirkstile

EWES CHURCH

Glendivan

Sorbie

Hoghill

Wrae

Flask

Bliss

Terrona

A7

N

Ewes Water

Langholm

MEMORIAL 32

*In memory of JOHN WHOTSON died in Wintershaugh June 6, 1768
aged 44 years   Likewise JOAN his daughter died October – 1769 aged
1 year   JAMES his son died November 5, 1769 aged 3 years   Also
JANE TELFER his spouse died at Craigs December 23rd 1823 aged
92 years*

Ewes Valley

BY JOHN ELLIOT, LANGHOLM

What is Ewes but a water clear,
That flows the green hills under,
Earth hath a thousand such elsewhere,
As worthy of our wonder?

ACH valley and watergate in this Borderland of ours has its own peculiar story and that of Ewes is well worth talking over. What can I say about Ewes except that it is on the road to Hawick? That may be so, but what stories were told of that same road in bygone times. Could I but conjure back to consciousness the men – drivers of the mail coaches, men like Sandie Elder of the Cross Keys, and old Govenlock of Mosspaul, or some of the carters and carriers of 100 years ago who travelled that road to Hawick – their tales would keep you interested all night, talks of robberies, accidents, hairbreadth escapes and adventures – adventures in coming down from Mosspaul when the drifting snow was blowing up the burn. Or could I recall to you the gossip collected by Tom Robson, the post runner, who "ran" with the letters from the Langholm and fished all the way up the Ewes – or of his successor, Willie Beattie, who was nearly done to death by highwaymen in the Wrae Wood, and later was accidentally shot while cleaning the pistol he carried for his own protection – then we would all realise that this same watergate of Ewes was alive with a human as well as an historic interest.

I have often applied to our watergate, too, what the poet said of Killarney. "Angels often pausing there doubt if Eden were more fair", for indeed on a summer morning the valley of Ewes is surpassing fair. It was perhaps this idea of Eden, or Paradise, that was in the mind of auld Chairlie Hope, one of the characters in Langholm just over 100 years ago. Chairlie's people were buried in Staplegordon and he imagined he had some grievance against a well-known family in Langholm for encroaching upon his grave space. He made the whole town ring with his tale of ill-treatment. One day, however, someone saw Chairlie at Staplegordon, building an archway in the stone dyke over the head of his wife's grave, and inquired what he was doing. "Oh well," said Chairlie, "it's for use on the Resurrection Morning, for the others'll be oot an' through Sorbie Hass afore the wife can climb the dyke." Evidently Chairlie thought the golden city with its streets so fair lay at the Ewes end of the Hass – surely a high compliment to the watergate of Ewes.

EWES AND LANGHOLM

But though the Ewes Valley may be the road from Langholm to Hawick it has nevertheless an individuality of its own and a place in history that is independent of its neighbours.

Langholm, for example, is only some 350 years of age. It was in 1621 that Maxwell received the Charter giving him the lands of Langholm and other places, and in 1628 the building of the town was begun. But Ewesdale, as a geographical division, has been known to history for 500 years and more. So that historically it is Langholm we have to relate to Ewes and not Ewes to Langholm. Indeed in Molls Map of 1745 Eskdale is not separately mentioned – the whole watershed is called Euesdaill.

The lands of Langholm formed part of the Regality of Eskdale which included the Baronies of Staplegordon, Langholm, Westerkirk, Canonbie, Tarras and the Tenandrie of Dumfedling. But Ewes, more definitely to the north of Arkin, was no part of these nor does there appear to have been a Barony of Ewes in the same sense as these other places. Indeed, Maxwell, who was Warden of the Marches, denied that Ewes came under his jurisdiction.

The lands in the watergate were granted by charter from time to time but there was no Baronial holding. This is a very important distinction and, it partly explains the present day feature of separate lairdships of Meikledale and Arkleton.

Perhaps the difference may be expressed in this way – that whilst Eskdale was feudal, Ewes was more under the rule of the Clan. Though there was no absolute baronial rule, there was an approach to it in the Tenandrie of Glenvorane corresponding to that of Dumfedling in Eskdale – where justice would be dispensed.

There was one fundamental difference, however, between Tweeddale and Eskdale: that of the jurisdiction of the superior. Under the Baronies, the superior had the right of pit and gallows, but no such power seems to have existed in Ewesdale, because in none of the charters relating to Ewes of the sixteenth century is there conferred the power of life and death.

CORN MILLS

There was another important difference between Ewesdale and Eskdale in the corn mills granted under the charters.

In the nine or ten miles from Langholm to the entrance to Mosspaul Burn there were mills at no fewer than six houses: Meikledale, Sorbie, Arkleton, Bliss, Glenvorane and Wrae. These appear to have been different from the mills in the Eskdale area in that they were not in any sense baronial mills to which the cultivators were "thirled".

Thirlage was one of the most objectionable and irritating feudal customs. It caused every farmer and every cultivator of the soil to regard the miller as his natural enemy. Oppression and favouritism were common and the miller had a hold over every cultivator and had the sanction and authority of the feudal lord behind him. Obviously with six mills in so limited an area no miller practised exactions such as were customary both as to charges and what were known as "multures" or "sequels".

According to the late Mr Robert Hyslop, joint author of *Langholm As It Was*, we have an excellent illustration of sequels in the Barley Bannock and the Salted Herring carried as emblems in the Common Riding procession. The miller, and later, the baron-bailie had the right to these sequels and the giving of these was resented by the tenants.

The Baronial Mill of Staplegordon was at Milnholm, and of Langholm at the Milltown at the foot of the Chapel Path.

SHIRES

At one time both Eusdale and Eskdale were within the Shire of Roxburgh – so says a Charter dated 1458 – but it is supposed that this is one of these misprints one sometimes finds in documents written at a considerable distance from the place, for only a few years later they are ascribed to Dumfries and continue so down through the sixteenth century.

In 1672, however, the Duke and Duchess of Buccleuch petitioned Parliament to have the five Eskdale parishes transferred to the County of Roxburgh for convenience of administration and this was granted. In Molls Map of 1745 both Ewes and Eskdale are shown as being in the County of Roxburgh, but only two years later, on the passing of the Heritable Jurisdiction Act in 1747 – an Act to rearrange and define the rights and privileges of the feudal superiors – the parishes were again restored to Dumfries. Had not this been done, I suppose we might easily have been described as Hawick folk.

But not only is Ewes separate and distinct in a geographical sense, it also has history and characteristics not shared by its neighbours.

RELICS

The oldest relic in the watergate, I suppose, is one which takes us back to before the period of written history, and is the stone known as the "Grey Wether", standing in front of Meikledale House.

Such stones are found here and there over Scotland and England, and in Scotland, at any rate, they are all known as "Wethers" – a derivation and meaning at which it is difficult to arrive. Some suppose they mark the burial place of some famous chief – others aver that they were objects of worship – but it is difficult to say.

Then one might mention the Turf Dyke running athwart the hills on the left bank of the Ewes an antiquity which interested so keenly the late Mr Matthew Welsh. Its purpose is one of those debatable themes, of which archaeology provides so many, but its similarity to the famous Catrail suggests a similar purpose.

Mention might be made also of the old British Camps scattered about the watergate – at Footsburn, Arkleton, Meikledale, Unthank and other places in Ewes.

There is one singularity of Ewes which is rather puzzling, and that is, that in the charters conveying lands in Eskdale and Wauchopedale there should so often be expressly reserved to the superior "the salmon and other fisheries of the Esk and Wauchope" – Ewes being left unmentioned.

There is only one charter in which the fisheries of Ewes are included – that of 1621 to the Earl of Nithsdale. Perhaps the reason lies in the fact that on the average the temperature of Ewes water is considerably

The Grey Wether

lower than that of Esk or Wauchope, but, of course, the fact remains that salmon do run in Ewes.

Would it be because of its lower temperature that the water of Ewes was chosen by the people of Langholm for the drowning of their witches – at a place called the "Grieve" which has never been properly identified but which is popularly supposed to be at its confluence with the Esk.

Talking about witches, there is a story told about a Minister of Ewes who was greatly annoyed by the too frequent visits to the Manse of one of his elders. The Minister tried as nicely as possible to discourage the visits but to no purpose. One night, on the elder going to pay his customary call, he found the Minister planting a rowan tree in the Manse garden.

> "So ye're planting a rowan tree to keep the witches away", said the elder. "Oh, no", said the Minister, "I've nee bother wi' the witches, it's something tee keep elders away I'm wanting".

EWES ROAD

The present road up Ewes Valley was constructed under a special Act of Parliament obtained in 1763 by Sir William Pulteney, Laird of Westerhall, and was completed some time prior to 1775. Up to the middle of the eighteenth century the road between Langholm and Hawick was little more than a bridle path, used mainly by packhorses travelling to and from England, hence communication between one town and another was very difficult. In these circumstances there could be but little commerce, and the comparatively small amount of merchandise carried was transported on horseback in creels slung across the animal's back. The use of packhorses was an absolute necessity, the road being ill-adapted even for them. Between the seventeenth and eighteenth centuries, the difficulty of finding any beaten track between Hawick and Langholm is seen from the following extracts taken from the Hawick Burgh records:

> "1651 . . . Robert Olipher, cordiner, was ardained to pay five pounds to the bailies for disobeying them, by refusing to go and act as guide to the English troopers to Langholm."

"1740 . . . Paid to Thomas Sword for being a guide to the Langholm with an officer of the dragoons, one shilling."

The approach to Ewes in the olden time was from Staplegordon by way of the desolate windings of Sorbie Hass, but on Langholm becoming a separate parish in 1703, the road was by way of the ford crossing at Ewes Foot, a short distance above the junction of the Ewes and Esk, then on towards the Chapel Path, and through the farm lands of Ba'gra to a point near Arkin, where the road came down to the present level. The Ba'gra Road was superseded in 1822 when the present road through Walker's Hole, and across the Tourneyholm was cut, and the bridge over the Ewes on the site of the High Mill was built.

The Miller's Hill – or Lamb Hill, as it is now called – previous to the cutting of the present road up the Ewes Valley by way of Kilngreen, sloped down to the banks of the river without an obstacle such as hedge or dyke in the way. At that period the Bar Wood was not yet planted. The road to Newcastleton was not yet formed but a road went up the Whitshiells as it now does, and a riding track from the farmhouse led over the hill-end into Tarras.

THE SIMMER FAIR

The Simmer Fair – now a thing of the past – was at that time a great event of importance in the neighbourhood. The Miller's Hill, the Kilngreen and sometimes up to the top of the Castle Hill were on these occasions literally covered with lambs, and buyers and sellers were to be numbered in scores. In his fascinating "Reminiscences", Simon Irving, of Langholm Mill, states that in his father's day the ground now occupied by the Langfauld Wood, and the Crofts, was the Staneholm Farm. This farm extended to the road above Langholm Corn Mill and was broken up by the Duke of Buccleuch when he was approached to grant stints to people in Langholm.

PERSONS

Another feature which distinguished Ewes was that the clans inhabiting it were different from those in Eskdale. Instead of the Thomsons, Glendinnings, Johnstones, Maxwells and Lindsays, Ewes had Littles,

Armstrongs, Elliots, Beatties and Scotts, not the Scotts of Buccleuch, but known in history as the "Scotts of Eusdaill" – of the Thirlestane and Howpasley branches.

Armstrongs

Armstrong and Elliot are name which occur again and again. Most of the strongholds in the watergate in the sixteenth and seventeenth

centuries were held by Armstrongs. As early as 1532, Ekke Armstrong occupied a place called Glengillis, and later Will Armstrong, who was a son of Hector of Liddesdale. In 1569 there were still Armstrongs there, who gave assurance for the Scotts of Ewesdale, and their name occurs as late as 1610 in this place. In 1569 Arkilton was occupied by George Armstrong, known as "Ninian's Geordie" – the Ninian referred to being at Park or Buss where the Armstrongs had been since 1535, and in 1605 Archie Armstrong was in Flaskholm. Sorbie was also in the possession of the Armstrongs and in the Kirkyard is a stone recording the death of John Armstrong of Sorbie, who died in 1685. The lands of Bliss, Howgill and Wrae were also occupied by Armstrongs.

Some of these Armstrongs derived from Armstrong of Barnglies who was a kinsman of the famous Johnnie of Gilnockie. There were also Armstrongs in Glendiven, Andrew Armstrong occupying this place in 1643.

Elliots

The Elliots of Ewesdale were of the Redheuch branch and were ancient allies of the Armstrongs, as the ballad says . . .

> The Elliots and the Armstrangs did convene
> They were a gallant companie:
> "We'll ryde and meit our lawful king
> And bring him safe to Gilnockie!"

In 1578 both Upper and Nether Fiddleton were occupied by an Elliot known as "Will o' Fiddleton". At the same time one Ringan – sometimes called Ninian – occupied Ewes Doors, and it indicates a sense of humour among them that he was known as "Ringan the Porter".

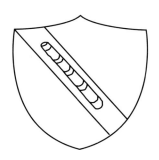

We also get Archie Elliot, son to Ringan's Will, the Porter and Hobbe of Glenvorane was an Elliot. In these descriptions Ewes Doors and Glenvorane seem to refer to the same holding or it was perhaps that Ewes Doors was the "friendly tenant" of Glenvorane, who was a holder of much importance. Everyone has heard of the famous fight between the Elliots and the Scotts in 1566. There had long been a feud between the two clans. The Elliots, led apparently by the Laird of Braidlie, to the number of 400 it is said, concentrated on Ewes Doors as the best strategical position. The battle was a sharp one and many of the Scotts were slain. The Armstrongs seem to have occupied Arkleton up to about 1610. By a charter dated 13 June 1611, the King granted the ten pound lands of Arkilton to William Elliot of Fallineske, and I think I am correct in saying that they have remained in the possession of that family since that date, though I believe it is also said that the Arkleton lands came to the Elliots by purchase from the Armstrongs.

Littles

The Littles are the oldest landed or tenant family in Ewesdale. As early as 1426 Simon Little was granted the lands of Meikledale, Sorbie and Kirktoun. There is an interesting stone in the Kirkyard recording the death of Thomas, the Laird's son, in 1673.

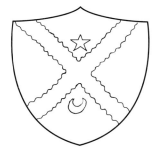

The Littles of Langholm are derived from this branch, one of the most influential men in Langholm being Bailie Little whose brother gave the name to the Laird's Entry.

Scotts

As already stated, the Scotts of Eusdaill were not the Scotts of Buccleuch but of Thirlestane. They were never very influential in Ewes though they contributed to a large extent to the disturbances on the Borders during the sixteenth century.

Someone has said that if you want to learn fully the history of the old Border families, you must search *Pitcairn's Criminal Trials*.

This certainly applies to the Scotts of Ewesdale. Among other exploits they took an active share in Morton's Raid of Stirling in 1578, also in the Raid of 1585, and several of their names appear in the list of those indemnified:

"Thomas Scott of Blackhall and John his son. Adam Scott in Mosspeeble and John his son. John, Geordie and Will Scott and Jock Scott in Arkleton."

The Scotts of Arkleton were not alone in that venture. There were with them the Armstrongs of Howgill, Ekke Armstrong of Gingles and his son, Sam Little of Meikledale, Thomas Armstrong of Wrae, in fact all the Scotts, Armstrongs and Littles of Ewesdale were in the ill-fated expedition. There seems no doubt that they were all ready to take their share in aiding Buccleuch to rescue Kinmont Willie some ten years later.

Buccleuch

The lands of Ewesdale came finally in 1643 to the Scotts of Buccleuch, excepting those Lairdships which had been granted, such as Arkleton and Meikledale.

It should be remembered that when the occupier is also proprietor the designation is "of", but when it is only a tenancy it is "in", so we speak of Elliot of Arkleton, Little of Meikledale, Armstrong of Sorbie, but of tenants we say Scotts in Arkleton, Armstrong in Glendiven, Elliots in Ewes Doors and so on, the difference being that the tenants occupied – the "laigh houses" which were an adjunct to the principal.

PLACES

Ewesdale began to appear in historical documents late in the thirteenth century and early in the fifteenth we have reference to the grant of the lands of Meikledale, Kirktoun and Sorbie. Throughout the sixteenth century there were frequent changes of ownership, lands being granted, "resigned", and again granted with puzzling frequency, the different owners including Avenels, Frasers, Lindsays, Earls of Mar, Home and Angus, Gideon Murray, Cranstoun, Nithsdale, and finally Buccleuch. It is very interesting to note the recurrence of the same place names again and again.

We have: Fiddleton, Blackshaw, Glenvorane (this was probably the most important of all the Ewesdale houses as it possessed the same feudal status as Dumfedling did in Eskdale that of a "free tenandrie", something lower than a Barony but greater than a mere house), Mosspaul, Mosspeeble, Unthank, Park of Buss, Sorbie, Meikledale, Gingillis, Howgill, Bliss, Flask or Flaskholm, Arkilton, Wrae, Terrona, and Glendiven.

These show an Ewesdale very similar in the distribution of places and population to what obtains today. These places, remember, were not twentieth-century bungalows but some of them, such as Glenvorane, Arkleton, and possibly Sorbie, were to some extent fortified houses as the "towers" were usually mentioned as being conveyed with the lands.

The name of Park is interesting. From about 1600 there are evidences of a change of name, as it is after that date always referred to as Park of Bus, or Buss, never as Bush. Probably the gradual anglification of our ancient Scots tongue accounts for this last form.

Terrona is not mentioned with the same frequency as some of the other houses and its form varies into names hardly recognisable. Apparently it was of less importance then than Flask, which is invariably given as Flask or Flaskholm, which, by the way, is the only occurrence of the Norse "holm" in higher Ewesdale.

The lands of Flask are sometimes referred to as extending "even to Terrona", so it must have been a holding of considerable extent.

Sorbie is one of the most interesting places in Ewes. The name occurs with some frequency in Scotland, and the north of England, indicating the Norse occupation; the "by" or "bie" meaning a habitation.

Associated with it is "Sorbie Hass". "Hass" is Norse for "throat" and when applied to a place means a narrow pass. So far as I am aware its association with the road from Staplegordon and Westerkirk into Ewes is the only use made of the word among local place names.

Frequently we get the same name for two places indicated by "Over" and "Nether". We have the Over-Kirk and the Nether Kirk of Ewes, Over and Nether Fiddleton, Bliss and Wrae.

Unthank is always referred to as Lands: the name is never applied to the Kirk. According to "Place Names of Dumfriesshire", by Colonel Johnson-Ferguson of Springkell, "the name Unthank denotes a piece of ground on which some squatter settled without leave of the lord".

Arkilton, under many different spellings, frequently occurs after 1530.

Gingillis. This is one of the most puzzling places in the watergate. I have no idea what it means but, in the fifteenth century, it was clearly a place of importance, and incidentally the fount and origin of many of the disturbances which gave Ewesdale a name on the Borders.

Meikledale, along with Arkilton, is one of the most famous of all the Houses in Ewesdale and seems to have preserved its identity from the early fifteenth century.

TOWERS

When reference is made to such places as "great houses", I have in mind the references in charters of the sixteenth century to the principal house on the lands being conveyed by the charters. For instance, you find granted the lands of Glenvorane "with the tower of Glenvorane to be the principal messuage", and the lands of Flask and Bliss "with their towers".

But not all of these places can have had strongholds such as we see in what remains of the old Border towers.

In Sandison's Map of the towers of the Debateable Land, dated 1590, the following are given in the watergate of Ewes: Tho of Zingles (shown on the opposite bank of the Ewes, but obviously referring to the same place which was later called Glingillis), Arkleton, Runion o' the Buss, Hobbe of Glenvorane.

At that period such houses were for the greater part built of wood, but some of those in Ewes were certainly of stone – remains having been found up the burn from Meikledale, whilst built into the present Mansion of Arkleton, I am told, are carved stones obviously from a former well-built house or tower, but gone beyond recall are many of the houses which were influential in Ewesdale 400 years ago.

Gone, too, are the days of romance when life on the Borders was an adventure – yes, if you like the days of raiding and reiving. State papers describe our ancestors as the "Ewesdale thieves", but remember that the men who called our ancestors thieves were probably themselves deeply implicated in the peculation of public money, for such was then the custom of officialdom.

It is quite true that life and conduct on both sides of the Border in the sixteenth century were not based on the Sermon on the Mount. As well say that our troops who adventured into shellfire and captured German guns and tanks were "stealing" them. The Borders were then in a condition of war and it is mere nonsense to apply to the sixteenth century a standard of conduct which is only painfully and unsuccessfully attempted in the twentieth.

KIRKS

There were three Kirks to serve the spiritual needs of Ewesdale before the Reformation. Unlike the Kirks of Eskdale, which were under the Abbey of Kelso, the Kirks of Ewes were under the Abbey of Melrose.

One was away up in Ewes Doors and was dedicated to St Paul, and one was at Unthank, though that name is never applied to it in documents. It is invariably referred to as the Over-Kirk of Ewes and was dedicated to St Mark, and the last was at Kirktoun known as the Lower or Nether-Kirk of Ewes and was dedicated to St Cuthbert.

We have scarcely any record of the incumbents of the Over-Kirk but one parson is mentioned as witnessing a document in the reign of Alexander the Third. There is a fairly reliable record of the Ministers of Nether Ewes from the end of the thirteenth century, but nevertheless the Over Kirk at Unthank appears to be the older foundation.

The association of the place name Unthank with the Over-Kirk of Ewes is interesting but puzzling. What the precise significance of the name of Unthank is, philologists seem unable to decide but, like that of Cross-Keys, it was generally associated with a religious foundation. The name is found in Cumberland, Durham, and several places in middle England, near Whitby and elsewhere, and its frequency indicates that it had a fairly general application.

The Over-Kirk of Ewes was abandoned at the Reformation. The watershed of the Esk is quite prolific in such derelict churches. We have also St Brides, near Westwater, and Wauchope; we have Watcarrick and Byken, in Eskdale, and Staplegordon, which makes six pre-Reformation Kirks abandoned. Of these, Staplegordon, which was under the Priory of Canonbie, was far the most important and famous.

The Nether-Kirk of Ewes stood on the site of the present building. Among its incumbents and Ministers were men of distinction whose memories are still honoured in the watergate. One might dwell a considerable time on the merits of John Lithgow, the Covenanter, who was deprived of the living by the Privy Council of 1664, but would not be disloyal to his conscience and so continued to preach in conventicles and had the "honour" of imprisonment on the Bass Rock.

Incidentally, one may remark that this same loyalty to Kirk and conscience must have been a characteristic of Ewes folk. There may be some alive still who can remember not a few out of Ewes who, according to their rights, refused to worship in the Established Kirk of Nether Ewes, but walked Sunday after Sunday to the Secession Kirk at the Townhead in Langholm.

The late Dr Joseph Brown used to tell a story of a shepherd and his wife, both ardent seceders, who travelled much the same distance. One day the wife went up to the husband who "walked on before" and in awe-struck tones enquired,

> "John, d'ye ken where the dog's been?" "No," said John, "where has it been?" "Weel", said the wife, "he ran up the steps o' the Auld Kirk and lookit in at the door."

The couple halted to review the serious situation implied by this announcement, then said Jen,

"What maun we dae, Jock?" "I'll tell ye what," was the reply, "We can dae nocht the day, seeing its the Sabbath, but we'll just wait till the morn and we'll shoot him."

But all the same, one must honour the men and women whose inspiring motive was loyalty to their Lord as they conceived their duty, and neither for fear nor favour would be disloyal to their consciences. It was this spirit that made Scotland great among the nations.

One could mention, too, and always with pride, the Rev. Robert Malcolm, grandfather of the four Knights of Eskdale. Mr Malcolm was presented to his charge by the Earl of Dalkeith, who also gave him the farm of Burnfoot, formerly named Cannel Shiels, at a nominal rent to help the stipend of Ewes which was at that time very small. Mr Malcolm was the founder of the Poor-house of Ewes.

One day the Poor-house was pointed out to an affluent business man from the North of England, who was so impressed with the beauty of its situation and appearance, and the peacefulness of its surroundings, that he asked to have his car stopped in order that he might make enquiries about rooms for his holidays.

Then many stories are told of the Rev. Robert Shaw, brother to the Rev. W. B. Shaw of Langholm. Like so many of the old Parish Ministers, Mr. Shaw had a keen sense of humour and greatly enjoyed a joke.

One very cold winter Sunday there was only one occupant of the gallery. Halfway through the sermon the worshippers were amazed to see him rise and address the Minister as follows:

"It's awfu' cauld up here, Mr Shaw, an' it'll be nee use bringing Wullie up here wi' the ladle, so there is ma penny." He birled the penny towards the pulpit and concluded by saying, "Now Aw propose we should sing a psalm and then have the Benediction."

On the occasion of a wedding of someone at the Kirkstyle, the giving in of the names provided a splendid and welcome excuse for some conviviality, and the Beadle was despatched to the Manse to crave from the Minister a bottle of whisky wherewith to celebrate the occasion.

"Whae's there?" Asked Mr Shaw.

"Oh," said the Beadle, "there's Jock so-and-so, an' Wullie so-and-so, an' Eck so-and-so."

"Oh," replied the Minister, "if Wullie's there, ye'll need mair than one bottle. Ye'd better take a couple," which he handed over to the surprised and gratified official.

In a lecture on Ewes given a good many years ago by one Mr James Graham, of Wishaw, he told how the old Kirk was thatched and that people who had brought themselves within the discipline of the Kirk were sent to collect heather and assist in mending the thatch, which strikes one as a very practical way of enjoining and exhibiting repentance.

THE BELL

The bell, which hangs on one of the trees in the Kirkyard, must be one of the most photographed bells in existence. Regular travellers on the Hawick to Langholm road were familiar with the sight of the old kirk bell fixed in the cleft of an ancient tree in the grounds of the kirk. Unfortunately, in the early 1950s, the tree had to be cut down owing to its condition. For a very short time the bell found rest in the vestry until another home could be secured for it.

Mr Kerr, the Minister, found the perfect solution by placing the bell in an adjacent tree which provided a suitable cleft. Now the bell is again restored to a tree and this interesting feature of Ewes Kirk is preserved.

No doubt you have heard the story of the wedding at Kirkstyle which was so tragically interrupted by the ringing of this self-same bell at dark midnight. Perhaps it might be worth telling again.

The fun was getting fast and furious when suddenly there was a toll of the bell. One or two people noticed it, but no one mentioned it and they went on with the dance. Another sharp toll at which womenfolk looked at one another a little scared. The men affected to make light of the incident and the merriment was resumed but in a more chastened spirit.

Again came the ominous sound – doubled in number and intensity. This could be ignored no longer. The dancing ceased and the more daring of the men volunteered to venture into the Kirkyard – dead of night though it was – and investigate this mysterious ringing of the bell. Just as they entered, however, there was heard a more clamant toll than ever and the men ran helter-skelter back to the house. Do not blame them, for these were the days of Burke and Hare and everything relating to the Kirkyard was eerie and regarded with fear and superstition. But their being safe in the house did not stop that fearsome ringing of the bell.

Consternation reigned and at last the company deemed it an occasion on which the aid of the Minister should be invoked. So a deputation set out to the Manse, and, rousing the Minister, they told him – what he himself could now hear – how the Kirk bell was being rung by unseen hands whose could be no other than Auld Nick himself.

The Minister reproved them for their foolish fears and, greatly to their comfort, volunteered to accompany them to ascertain the cause of this unseemly occurrence.

They had got to the brig over the Kirktoun Burn when there was another series of loud and insistent peals. They looked to the Minister – but he was down on his knees saying, "Let us pray" – after which they betook themselves to the wedding. All the long dread night that bell kept ringing and finally, when day dawned, there was eager anxiety to ascertain the cause.

It was then discovered that someone had maliciously tethered the Minister's goat to the bell rope hanging loose from the tree, and every movement of the goat straining at the tether caused the bell to toll.

Great was the indignation at the Kirkstyle, but the culprit was not discovered until many years later, when a well-set-up man visiting his native valley from America, made the astounding confession that he was the scamp who had done this scandalous thing.

The Kirkyard contains many interesting memorial stones on which are found the clan names of the Ewes Valley and of the neighbouring districts: Littles, Armstrongs, Scotts, Jacksons, Rutherfords, Borthwicks, Beatties, Malcolms and Aitchisons. On the family stone of the Malcolms appear the names of three of the Knights of Eskdale, although, of course, Sir John is not actually buried there.

Another stone has the following inscription:

> "Here lyes Christopher Holiday son to John Halliday who died on the 23 day of December 1747 returning home from Carlisle in company with Adam Graham, was on the Beck Moor, near Bating-bush, treacherously assaulted by the said Adam, who shot him in at the back and with his gun staff, made wounds in the head and there after *robbed*(?) him, he died of his wounds the 5 day after, in the 40th year of his age."

When my attention was drawn to this stone by Mr Slack and I read the inscription, I thought I had discovered an incident which had hitherto escaped all the chroniclers of Langholm and district because, at the first glance, I came to the conclusion that the Beck Moss mentioned on the stone was simply a misspelling and that Becks Moss was really the locus of the crime. However, the murder appears to have been committed in the Longtown district because Baiting Bush is near to Glenzierbank and there is a Beck Moss there, too.

While on the subject of stones, one might mention a stone which is placed on the summit of a precipitous slope on the Buss heights. The stone, which I believe has fallen down recently, was placed there to commemorate a daring piece of horsemanship, or, I should say, horsewomanship. The inscription on the stone is as follows:

> "This stone commemorates Lady Florence Cust's daring ride straight down this brae with the Eskdale Hounds, 20th February, 1861."

IN SCOTLAND

It is curious that both Canonbie and Ewes had to fight for their inclusion in the Kingdom of Scotland.

In 1482, the Duke of Albany, uncle of James I, who had granted Meikledale, Sorbie and Kirktoun to Simon Lytel, thought to seize the Scottish Crown, and, in return for English support, he offered to barter away the nationality of this watergate by ceding Ewes to England.

In the days when Scottish and English Commissioners were determining the limits of the Debateable Land, the English wardens claimed Canonbie as English. The Canonbie people strongly objected to this and absolutely refused to pay the tribute to England, declaring that they were Scots and had always been Scots, all except Prior John, who claimed Scottish nationality, but at the same time gave assurances to the English warden, like the famous Vicar of Bray.

Ewes, too, had a narrow escape, though had the worst then happened, the patriotism of the clans of Ewes would have rectified the blunder of their lord superior.

Powerful indeed is the tenacity with which our affections cling to Scotland. It is said that we are blind to its faults – possibly we are.

You remember that in one of his whimsicalities, Barrie tells of going to a bookseller's and asking for a book about Scotland but one which did not always praise Scotland and the Scots but showed their "faults". The bookseller stared at him and then inquired, "What faults?"

The late Ian Maclaren was lecturing once in New York and, at the conclusion of his address, a tall and strapping Highlander was shown into his room and exclaimed: "Man, we're a wonderful nation." The lecturer hinted at a few of the national failings, and the Highlander listened to the end and then, waving his hand, he said: "Man, they're never worth mentioning, never worth mentioning."

And today we too are loath to admit them, for Scotland is our home and its men and women are oor ain folk.

EWES MEN

Matthew Welsh

I have hinted that Ewes deserves some of the fame attaching to celebrated men of Eskdale – like the Malcolms. But a man may well come within the category of greatness who never won a title or even popular recognition. When I think of the men whom this watergate of Ewes has produced, my mind goes at once to the late Matthew Welsh, a real hero in homespun. On consideration now – remember I was but a boy when Matthew Welsh, an old man, died – I do not think I could picture a man whom I would take to be so representative of the solid character and intelligence of the Scottish peasantry.

Reading the inscription on his tomb, I could not help repeating:

> "Perhaps in this neglected spot is laid
> Some heart once pregnant with celestial fire . . ."

For Matthew Welsh was no mere "mute, inglorious Milton". I could fancy that it would not be difficult to be a poet if you lived in this beautiful valley, and Matthew Welsh's poetic instincts were nurtured on the scenery and the story of the watergate of Ewes. I do not claim that his work will live – who reads Matthew Welsh now-a-days? - nor would I say that his work touched any high mark of poetic expression, but he sang just because he must and his poetry gave much pleasure to those who read it as it did to him in writing it.

William Knox

It has always been a matter of surprise to me that more value has not been placed locally upon the work of William Knox, at one time tenant of the Wrae. Truly he was not an Ewes man by birth, but I have no doubt that its great natural beauty inspires his muse. His poems are for the most part religious, and one of their defects is the "fleeting scene" outlook they afford of life and destiny. But, apart from this motive, his poem on "Mortality", written by a young man in his thirties, when optimism ought to be his dominating note, is a piece of very beautiful work viewed from a literary standpoint. As no doubt you know, this poem was a favourite with the great American, Abraham Lincoln, who had it printed and hung in his study, a fact which was urged by those who claimed him wrongly as the author of the poem.

Henry Scott Riddell

But, in thinking of poetry associated with Ewes, one's mind goes at once to Henry Scott Riddell, born at Sorbie, right in the centre of the watergate. If Henry Scott Riddell had never written another poem other than "Scotland Yet", this would entitle him to a place in the Temple of Fame. "Scotland's howes and Scotland's knowes" – I think that phrase is photographic of the valley of Ewes. The song, "Scotland Yet", is one of the finest songs of patriotism ever penned and amongst Scotsmen, the world over, stands second only to "Auld Lang Syne", and when we sing it we are proud of the valley of the Ewes which gave it birth.

As one thinks of the charming scenery of Ewesdale inspiring poetic expression, it is interesting to speculate as to what would have happened had the Waverley Line come up Ewes instead of Liddesdale, as was at one time likely. Possibly Ewes would have become a bungalow town for the man of toil and care in the city crowd of Langholm, but perhaps it is good that the railway has not changed the valley. Ewes is still rural and pastoral, but had the railway been built we might have had railway sidings on the Flaskholm and a signal box looking into Unthank Kirkyard.

President Roosevelt

It is not generally known that the late President Roosevelt had in his veins the blood of a famous Scottish Border family, and a connection with the Ewes Valley. Roosevelt was very proud of this connection. In fact he called his favourite terrier "Falla", after the home of his remote Scottish ancestors, the Murray's of Falla. He is a direct descendant of the "Outlaw Murray", the hero of a celebrated ballad which was included by Sir Walter Scott in his *Minstrelsy of the Scottish Border*. One of the Murray's became the tenant of the farm of Unthank in Ewes. After settling there he married Barbara Bennet, a daughter of the Laird of Chesters, a small estate near Ancrum. To the union there were born five children of whom James, the eldest, was destined to be the channel for the bringing of the blood of the "Outlaw Murray" into the Roosevelt family. His father, John Murray, died in 1728, at the early age of 51, leaving his widow and family badly provided for. Four years later, the lease of the farm was taken off the widow's hands by Walter Scott (an uncle of Sir Walter) and Robert Elliot, and her two boys had to begin to make their way in the world.

James Murray determined to try his fortune in the New World and in 1735, he embarked for Charleston in South Carolina and ultimately he became a very important personage in the colony. He became involved in the War of Independence and he went to Boston which was occupied by the British troops. When General Howe decided upon its evacuation, Murray sailed to Halifax in Nova Scotia, where he died in 1781. His two daughters had both married supporters of the revolutionary cause. The younger married Edward Hutchison Robbins and their third daughter, christened Anne Jean, married a Joseph Lyman and, a generation later, their daughter, Catherine Robbins Lyman, married a Mr Warren Delano, and one of their children was Sara Delano, who by her marriage to James Roosevelt became the mother of Franklin Delano Roosevelt. There is no broken link in the line of pedigree between the former farmer of Unthank and the late President of the United States, and that forms yet another factor which makes the watergate of Ewes such an interesting place.

MOSSPAUL

I have purposely left Mosspaul as the last of my references in the watergate. In fact one could give a lecture on the subject of Mosspaul alone, as this famous hostelry comes frequently into the picture of the old coaching days and is full of traditional lore. So far as can be traced, the earliest mention of the Inn is to be found in the autobiographical writing of Dr Carlyle of Inveresk, an eminent personage and one of the leaders of the church in his day. Travelling towards Langholm, he passed down the Ewes Valley in the year 1767, driving in his open chaise, accompanied by his wife and one or two friends, including the parish Ministers of Hawick. According to Dr Carlyle, the landlord of Mosspaul at this time was one Rob Achison, but, in contradistinction to this, the late Mr. James Edgar, who addressed the members of Hawick Archaeological Society in 1933 on the subject of "Mosspaul and its Historical Associations", stated that the first landlord of whom any record can be traced was a Thomas Gray, whose name appeared on a list in 1803 as one of those who were prepared to defend their country against the threatened French invasion.

Probably the most noted visitor to enter Mosspaul was Sir Walter Scott. It was in the autumn of 1792 that Sir Walter, then a young advocate, entered the Ewes Valley for the first time, accompanied by his great friend, Sheriff Shortreed. Previous to this, Scott and his friend, in their search for material for the *Minstrelsy of the Scottish Border*, had visited Liddesdale – Sir Walter's coach being the first wheeled vehicle ever to be seen in that district – and they met the famous Willie Elliot of Millburnflat, the original of Dandie Dinmont, who incidentally is supposed to have been buried in Unthank Kirkyard. Further down the Ewes Valley lived old Laird Beattie of Meikledale, who, it is said, supplied Scott with much of his information about Eskdale. Certainly it was Beattie who was responsible for the introduction of Gilpin Homer of Todshawhill into the epic tale of the *Lay of the Last Minstrel.*

Other famous visitors to Mosspaul included the poet Wordsworth and his sister Dorothy, while the great statesman William Ewart Gladstone and his wife, in their young days, frequently spent a night at this well-known hostelry.

The name Mosspaul is understood to be of ancient origin, and it is mentioned in the charters of the Earl of Home in the beginning of the sixteenth century but, curiously enough, it is not mentioned in Blaeu's Map, nor is the Kirk of St Paul in Ewes Doors.

Possibly the most famous landlord of Mosspaul was Robert Govenlock, an uncle of my grandfather, who, coming to Mosspaul in 1816, continued as landlord for forty-five years. He was for several years a guard on the mail coach, and was a picturesque figure in his official scarlet coat, top boots and hat trimmed with gold braid. Nine and a half hours were allowed for the journey of the coach between Edinburgh and Carlisle, the distance being scheduled as 95 miles. After Govenlock, who was familiarly known as "Gloomy Winter", became landlord, many additions and improvements were made to the hotel but the coming of the railway marked the beginning of the famous Inn's closing days and after 1864 the licence was allowed to lapse. For a number of years the place was occupied as a private dwelling, but afterwards it fell into a ruinous condition.

The advent of the cycle created a desire for the resuscitation of Mosspaul and in January 1900, a company was formed in Hawick and, as a result, the present building was erected and opened on the 7 July 1900. A crowd numbering several hundreds was present at the ceremony and among the first to drive up to the front door was old Sandy Elder of the Cross Keys, Canonbie, who was at that time 80 years of age, but, nevertheless, he handled the reins of his four-in-hand with the same dexterity as he did when, as a young man, he drove the mail coach up the self same road.

Intimately connected with Mosspaul was the renowned Wisp Club, which took its name from the hill which rises immediately behind the hotel to a height of 1,950 feet above sea level. The Club, which was composed of the principal farmers in the district, was formed in the spring of 1826, and it was resolved that the members should dine annually in Mosspaul on the Friday after Dumfries Spring Horse Market and record the average prices obtained the previous season for one and two years old Galloway cattle, all descriptions of Cheviot and Blackfaced sheep, and their respective wools, produced in Scotland south of the Firth of Forth. I might mention one of the resolutions adopted by the Club. This is Rule 2: "That no person after 1828 will be admitted a member of the Club unless regularly proposed and voted in by two-thirds of the members of the Club present, and that no person will be considered worthy of this Society unless he be able to drink one bottle of whisky."

Amongst the original members of the Wisp Club were two farmers from Ewes: Alexander Pott, Burnfoot, and Robert Scott, Eweslees, and it might also be mentioned that the second landlord of the present hotel when it opened in 1900 was Mr William Allen, now of Charles Street (New), Langholm.

2

Memorials in Ewes Churchyard

1   In memory of ARTHUR FOSTER who died at Langholm April 15th 1803 aged 78 years   Also ANNE PARK his spouse who died 22nd May 1821 aged 95 years   Also ANNE FOSTER their daughter who died November 22nd 1822 aged 53 years Also ARTHUR FOSTER their son who died March 29th 1823 aged 44 years (Inscribed on reverse) In memory of JOHN FORESTER [sic] interred at Castletown he died in 1727 aged (uncut)   Also KATHRIN HENDERSON in Effgill his relict who died July 31st 1756 (66?) aged 66 years   Also their daughter DOROTHA who died September 28th 1748 aged 21 years

2   In memory of ISABEL GRAHAM spouse to James Thomson who died at Linehope January 23rd 1817 aged 43 years   Also JEAN their daughter who died September 21st 1816 aged 23 years   Also JAMES their son who died March 1st 1817 aged 22 years   And MARY who died July 28th 1817 aged 17 years   Also 3 sons and 2 daughters who died in infancy. And MARGARET who died April 26th 1819 aged 19 years

3   In memory of ROBERT ARMSTRONG, Shepherd died at Meikledalehope 11th April 1832 aged 34 years   Also

CHRISTIAN LITTLE his wife died 4th July 1878 aged 82 years   Also SIMON their son died 16th February 1833 aged 5 months (damaged stone)

4   To the memory of THOMAS GRAHAM son of William Graham and Jane Hope, Milnholm, he died 15th June 1849 aged 22 years   Also JAMES their son who died in infancy   Also JANE HOPE spouse of William Graham who died at Milnholm 4th July 1856 aged 55 years

5   To the memory of JANET ARMSTRONG wife of George Armstrong, Burnfoot, Eskdale who died 16th September 1861 aged 65 years JOHN ARMSTRONG their son who died 29th August 1846 in his 22nd year THOMAS their son died 4th July 1829 aged 18 months   Also the above GEORGE ARMSTRONG who died there 4th June 1881 aged 77 years Also HELEN their daughter who died at Dumfries 14th February 1905 aged 69 years

6   In memory of THOMAS JACKSON shepherd who died at Howgill June 26th 1852 aged 49 years   Also MARY SCOTT his wife who died in New Langholm 27th February 1871 aged 63 years   Also two children who died in infancy   Also MARGARET their daughter who died in New Langholm July 24th 1856 aged 17 years THOMASINA their daughter who died 25th November 1868 aged 25 years

7   In memory of WILHELMINA BEATTIE spouse to John Scott Shepherd, at Muckledalehaugh who died January 18th 1800 aged 23 years

8   Here lies JOHN SCOTT in Cronksbankhead died 18th August 1734 aged 56 years   Also ISABEL SCOTT his spouse died 12th April 1752 aged 65 years   Also THOMAS SCOTT of

Cooms their son died 17th April 1768 aged 61 years   Also JEAN VEITCH his spouse died at Brierryshaw 25th March 1814 aged 95 years   Also JOHN WILLIAM and THOMAS their children died in infancy   Also JOHN LITTLE SCOTT their grandson who died there 1st February 1809 aged 10 years Also ISABELLA SCOTT their daughter who died there 11th March 1826 aged 72 years   Also JAMES SCOTT their son who died there 6th April 1825 aged 82 years   Also JANE OGILVIE his spouse died there 13th April 1800 aged 44 years Also JANE SCOTT their daughter died there 8th June 1847 aged 67 years   Also JESSIE SCOTT their daughter died at Briery Shaw Cottage May 3rd 1864 aged 75 years

9   In memory of JAMES MITCHEL died in Drummond Hall 28th January 1795 aged 74 years   Also JEAN BEATTIE his spouse died 18th August 1812 aged 90 years   Also THOMAS his son died aged 19 years   Also JEAN his daughter died aged 27 years (no dates given)   Also their granddaughter JEAN MITCHEL died 22nd September 1808 aged 16 years   Also JANET MITCHEL died July 15th 1823 aged 67 years

10   To the memory of HEUGH COWAN son to Robert Cowan in Lieheds died February 15th 1780 aged 14 years   Also MARGRAT his daughter died August 12th 1780 aged 17 years 3 children died in infancy   Also the said ROBERT COWAN died at Langholm August 6th 1801 aged 84 years

11   Here lyes ANDREW TURNBULL in Kirton died July 15th 1760 aged 61 years And JEAN CORIE his spouse died September 14th 1788 aged 74 years

12   In memory of JOHN ARMSTRONG who died at Langholm 30th October 1814 aged 60 years   Also ELIZABETH PATTERSON his wife who died at Langholm 10th January 1822 aged 65 years   Also ISABELLA DODDS wife of William Armstrong who died at Caulfield 17th February 1869 aged 77

years   Also the said WILLIAM ARMSTRONG who died at Langholm 31st May 1876 aged 79 years

13   In memory of JAMES RODGER died at Cairwoodrigg 9th January 1837 aged 39 years   Also ISABLE [*sic*] NICHOL his spouse who died at Cairwoodrigg 17th May 1834 aged 28 years And their children JAMES RODGER who died at Cairwoodrigg 4th November 1827 aged 15 months   Also ELIZABETH who died November 11th 1837 aged 9 years

14   In memory of JOHN TELFORD shepherd who died at Arkletonshiel on the 24th day of May 1847 aged 88 years Also MARY DOUGLAS his spouse who died at Longhouse, Parish of Falstone, County of Northumberland on the 8th day of January 1817 aged 65 years   Also of their son JOHN TELFORD shepherd who died at Newcastleton 17th day of March 1855 aged 66 years   Also ELIZABETH TELFORD their daughter who died at Newcastleton 1st September 1868 aged 72 years (inscribed on reverse : Earth is no loss but neither gain to those who life by death obtain)

15   In memory of ARTHUR HENDERSON died in Arkleton June 4th 1783 aged 62 years   Also JEAN GLENDINNING his wife died December 31st 1790 aged 76 years   Also the children of John Henderson and Elizabeth Elliot MARGARET who died March 2nd 1790 aged 2 years and of ARTHUR who died April 23rd 1796 aged 11 years   Also of the said JOHN HENDERSON teacher in Wauchope died July 18th 1823 in the 71st year of his age

16   Here lyes MARGRET LITL spouse to James Henderson who died in February 1688 hir age 51 JAMES HENDERSON aged 75 (no date inscribed)

17   In memory of HENRY HALLIBURTON, Shepherd who died at Howpasley died 27th March 1812 aged 66 years

18   In memory of WILLIAM HENDERSON died at Limeycleugh
      January 10th 1816 aged 89 years Likewise HELEN SCOTT his
      spouse died 4th February 1810 (no age given)

19   (Reverse of 18) In memory of MARY SMITH spouse to William
      Henderson, Cooms, she died 15th February 1782 aged 60
      years   Also their daughter ELIZABETH died 11th February
      1778 aged 25 years   Also FRANCIS their son died 15th April
      1779 aged 24 years

20   In memory of JAMES LITTLE in ____ died December 30th 1778
      aged 7? years   Also ELIZABETH his daughter died 28th
      December 1783 aged __ years   Also ELIZABETH died in
      infancy (Stone badly worn)

21   Here lyes CHRISTOPHER HOLIDAY son to John Halliday who
      died on the 23 day of December 1747 returning home from Carlisle
      in company with Adam Graham, was on the Beck Moor, near
      Bating-bush, treacherously assaulted by the said Adam, who shot
      him in at the back and with his gun staff, made wounds in the
      head and there after ____ him, he died of his wounds the 5 day
      after, in the 40th year of his age

22   (Reverse of 21) Here lyes JOHN HALLIDAY son to William
      Halliday in Pethers Wals who died June 2 1746 ? aged 2
      months

23   In memory of WILLIAM HOLLIDAY portioner in Langholm died
      at Wiffingham, County of Durham in October 1759 aged 50
      years   Also MARGARET ROSS his spouse died at Langholm
      November 3rd 1790 aged 77 years   Also MARGARET
      HOLLIDAY their daughter died December 27th 1827 aged 73
      years

24   In memory of JOHN SMITH died at Howpasley 18th June 1797
      aged 75 years

25 Here lyes WILLER WILSON weaver in Mosnubels [sic] (Mosspeebles?) July 1714 aged (uncut) years JEAN BYERS his spouse April 29, 1752 aged 62 years Likewys MARGRAT their daughter Agust 27, 1750, 26

26 In memory of ROBERT ELLIOT in Sorbie died February 24, 1773 51 years MARY ELLIOT his daughter died December 4, 1788 aged 17 years   Also JANET WILSON his spouse died September 4, 1780 aged 63 years   Also JOHN ELLIOT died March 10, 1792   aged 25 years

27 Interred the body of ROBERT ELLIOT carrier died at Arcin [sic] 7th May 1795 aged 33 years

28 In memory of THOMAS ARMSTRONG of Sorbie who died May 14th 1761 aged 81 years Here lyeth JEAN ELLIOT spouse to Thomas Armstrong of Sorbie who died July 24th 1734 aged 51 years   Also WILLIAM ARMSTRONG their son who died July 31st 1782 aged 72 years   Also GEORGE ARMSTRONG his son who died January 21st 1774 aged 23 years   Also HELIN [sic] ELLIOT spouse to the said William Armstrong she died June 11th 1790 aged 72 years   Also THOMAS son to above Thomas Armstrong who died at Sorbie 31st July 1758 aged 43 years   Also CHRISTIAN ELLIOT his spouse who died at Rickerton Mill 9th June 1790 aged 61 years

29 In memory of HELEN HUTTON wife of William Lauder who died at Arkleton 18th November 1866 aged 37 years   Also ALISON their daughter who died 24th October 1860 (or 69) aged 11 years   Also the said WILLIAM LAUDER who died at Arkleton 13th September 1880 aged -7 years   Also HELEN their daughter who died at Langholm —December 1907 aged 46 years (stone in two pieces deeply embedded and badly worn)

30 In memory of HENRY ANDERSON, shepherd who died at Riggfoot 13th February 1868 aged 57 years   Also

MARGARET THOMPSON his wife who died at Greenbank Cott 16th February 1899 aged 86 years   Also WALTER ANDERSON their son who died at Shielswood 20th September 1907 aged 65   Also HENRY ANDERSON their son who died at Hawick 29th August 1912 aged 54 years   Also MARGARET their daughter who died at Hawick 29th December 1925 aged 81 years

31   Here lyes MR. ROBERT DARLING, Minister of the Gospel at this place. He was ordained November 20th 1694. He dyed December 1716 and of his age 47 years. Here lyes   Also several children (See Notes)

32   In memory of JOHN WHOTSON died in Wintershaugh June 6, 1768 aged 44 years Likewise JOAN his daughter died October— 1769 aged 1 year JAMES his son died November 5, 1769 aged 3 years   Also JANE TELFER his spouse died at Craigs December 23rd 1823 aged 92 years

33   Here lyeth WILLIAM CARMICHAEL, Minister of the Gospel at Wamphray and Athelstanefoord and Mekerstoun for 45 years _____ Epitaph _____ he was deprived for refusing to swear the test and died in 1718 in the 72nd year of his age Here also lye JAN JOHNSTOUN his spouse who died 1719 of age 70 years MARY CARMICHAEL spouse to Th. Melvill in Blackhall who died 1715 of age 37 years and five of her children. HEL. DOUGLASS [sic] his grandchild daughter of Mr. Archibald Douglass, Minister Saltoun died 1719 of age 24 years.   Also GRIZEL MALCOLM sister to Mr Robert Malcolm, Minister of the Gospel in this place who died in 1719 of age 34 years

34   In memory of JOHN HYSLOP tenant in Arkin died July 12th 1806 aged 86 years   Also JANET HOTSON his spouse died April 14th 1775 aged 49 years   Also 4 of their sons – WALTER died in Dalkeith and is interred there – ANDREW, JOHN and WILLIAM died at sea

35   Here lyes JEAN HUTTAN spouse to George Wilson in Howgill
      who died 6th April 1769 aged 50 years

36   In memory of WILLIAM MURRAY who died at Brownhills 23rd
      July 1886 aged 90 years   Also JANET JACKSON his wife
      who died there 21st October 1879 aged 80 years   Also JOHN
      MURRAY their son who died at Enzieholm 29th April 1879 aged
      39 years   Also MARGARET MURRAY their daughter who
      died at White Castles 10th October 1839 aged 6 years

37   In memory of HELEN CORRIE wife of Walter Scott who died at
      Langholm 10th July 1884 aged 62 years   Also THOMAS
      JOSEPH their son who died 6th May 1885 aged 22 years
      Also the above WALTER SCOTT who died 15th December 1890
      aged 82 years   Also ELIZABETH SCOTT their daughter who
      died 5th August 1907 aged 61 years   Also MARGARET
      SCOTT their daughter who died at Langholm 6th February 1939
      aged 95 years

38   Here lyes JOHN BELL, smith in Kirkstile husband to Janet Lamb
      died upon the 8 day of May 1713 and of age 33

39   In memory of WILLIAM MURRAY who died at Broombraefoot
      1st February 1818 aged 69 years   Also JANE LITTLE his
      spouse died September 18th 1815 aged 81 years   Also SIMON
      MURRAY son to William Murray who died at Carretrigg
      September 6th 1805 aged 28 years   Also THOMAS
      MURRAY son to William Murray who died June 19th 1813 aged
      34 years

40   (Reverse of 39) In memory of VIOLET MURRAY daughter of
      William Murray and wife of Adam Paterson who died at Bailliehill
      7th April 1855 aged 80 years

41   In memory of WILLIAM LITTLE in Nether Barrascroft who
      died   February 1792 in the – year of his age

42   Here lie earthly remains of the REV MR ROBERT MALCOLM
      the worthy Pastor of this Parish who by a wise blameless pious
      and ami-able behaviour in private life acquired the esteem of all
      and supported the proper dignity of the sacred character which
      he continued uniformly to adorn by an able and diligent attention
      to the important duties of it through the course of a faithful and
      useful ministry from the 29th August 1717 to the 14th March
      1761 when he went hence to receive the reward of his labour in
      the Lord aged 74 and near to the body of her husband be also the
      remains of AGNES CAMPBELL his affectionate spouse and
      companion through life who surbiving him a few years 9th day
      of August 1767 aged 78 years Erected to dear venerable memory
      of his respectable parents by George Malcolm only surviving son
      (See Notes)

43   Sacred to the memory of GEORGE MALCOLM son of the Rev.
      Robert Malcolm, Minister of this Parish who died at Burnfoot,
      Westerkirk, 13th May 1803 aged 74 years   Also to the
      memory of MARGARET wife of George Malcolm daughter of
      James Pasley, Esq. of Craig she died 9th November 1811 aged 69
      years   Also in memory of their children MAGDALENE who
      died at Burnfoot 23rd September 1779 aged 17 years   Also
      CHARLOTTE an infant who died 19th September 1779
      Also GEORGE a mid-shipman Royal Navy, who died at Cape
      Nicolamole 29th January 1794 aged 18 years   Also
      WILLIAM who died at Burnfoot 19th March 1804 aged 22
      years   Also THOMAS, a merchant, who died at Madras 25th
      July 1809 aged 39 years (See Notes)

44   (Cont. on another face of tomb) GILBERT, M.A. Rector in
      Todenham who died here 16th April 1855 aged 79 years   Also
      HELEN ELPHINSTONE who died at Burnfoot 29th December
      1858 aged 87 yrs   Also STEPHAN [sic] who died at Burnfoot
      26th November 1861 aged 87 years Also MARGARET daughter
      of Sir James Malcolm, K.C.B. who died at Milholm February
      17th 1887 aged 75 years

45   (Cont. on another face of tomb) ROBERT, E.I.C. Civil Service
      who died at Burnfoot 2nd October 1813 aged 49 years   Also
      DAVID, Merchant, who died at Bombay 29th January 1826
      aged 47 years   Also WILHELMINA who died at Burnfoot
      3rd August 1832   aged 66 years   Also JOHN
      Major-General, E.I.C. Service, G.C.B. K.L.S. F.R.S. who died in
      London 3rd May 1833 aged 64 years   Also AGNES who
      died at Irvine 20th April 1836 aged 73 years   Also
      MARGARET widow of John Briggs, Esq. Barrister-at-law,
      who died at Burnfoot 10th March 1838 aged 64 years   Also
      PULTENEY, Admiral of the Blue, G.C.B. G.C.M.G. who died at
      East Lodge, Middlesex, 20th July 1838 aged 70 years   Also
      JAMES, Lieut.-Colonel, Royal Marines K.C.B. who died at
      Milnholm 27th December 1849 aged 82 years   Also
      CHARLES, Vice-Admiral, Knight, who died at Brighton 14th June
      1851 aged 68 years

46   In memory of WILLIAM ELLIOT mason in Langholm died 5th
      December 1825 aged 72 years   Also JANE DAVIDSON his
      wife died 29th January 1827 aged 75 years   Also MATTHEW
      ELLIOT their son died 8th July 1792 aged 10 months   Also
      JANE BEATTIE ELLIOT their daughter died 14th January
      1805 aged 7 years and 11 months   Also REV. WILLIAM
      ELLIOT their son, curate of Woolford in County of Warwick
      and formerly Purser Royal Navy died 13th October 1822 aged
      33 years and was buried in the churchyard at Woolford .   Also
      REV. JOHN ELLIOT A.M. their son, Minister at Peebles died
      April 28th 1847 in the 60th year of his age and in the 22nd year
      of his ministry

47   Sacred to the memory of GILBERT ARMSTRONG surgeon who
      died at Langholm September 27th 1796 aged 32 years   Also
      DAVID ARMSTRONG who died in the Congo May 10th 1796
      aged 28 years   Also ALEXANDER ARMSTRONG who died
      at Whidaw, December 1st 1799 aged 38 years Both on the Coast
      of Africa

48 Sacred to the memory of ROBERT HYSLOP, tenant Fairneyhirst and Airkin died at Airkin 8th October 1807 aged 52 years Also JEAN OLIVER his spouse interred in Stow Churchyard died at Cattleshiel 8th June 1852 aged 84 years. Also JOHN HYSLOP their son died in infancy. The following are interred in Stow Churchyard : MARGARET HYSLOP their daughter died in Stobshiel 10th March 1827 aged 32 years THOMAS HYSLOP their son, surgeon in Gifford died 8th September 1834 aged 28 years ROBERT HYSLOP their son tenant Stobshiel and Cattleshiel died at Cattleshiel 14th September 1844 aged 44 years In memory of MARY HYSLOP daughter of John Hyslop late in Arkin died August 8th 1819 aged 60 years

49 In memory of JOHN PARK died at Westwater 11th November 1800 in the 83rd year of his age Also ISABEL PARK his spouse died 1st April 1805 in the 79th year of her age WALTER PARK their son died 7th November 1760 in the 19th year of his age

50 In memory of ANN HUTTON spouse of John Ure she died at Meiledalehaugh 23rd April 1831 aged 31 years Also ELIZABETH URE their daughter died at Milnholm 28th July 1836 aged 15 years. 3 of his children died in infancy

51 Here lyes ROBERT LAIDLOW leat (late) herd in Glendinning 9th August 1755 aged 35 years their son WILLIAM LAIDLOW died at Rigg October 8 1775 aged 23 years And JOHN BEATTIE died in Langholm 5th September 1812 (no age cut) Also ELIZABETH SCOTT his wife died 24th June 1865 aged 79 years Also JOHN BEATTIE their son who died 5th February 1875 aged 65 years

52 (Reverse of 51) Erected to the memory of ROBERT LAIDLOW mason who died at Glendining 6th August 1770 in the 20th year of his age

53   In memory of ARCHIBALD LITTLE who died at Kilncleugh died August 6th 1843 aged 82 years   Also CATHARINE NICOL his spouse who died at Arasgill, August 20th 1796 aged 33 years   Also SIMON LITTLE their son aged 10 years   Also GEORGE aged 18 months   Also JANE their daughter in Langholm died August 25th 1864 aged 73 years

54   To the memory of JOHN YOUNG died at Sandyhaugh 22nd January 1789 aged 80 years MALLY LAIDLAW his wife died at Kirkstile 9th September 1797 aged 82 years Likewise their son WILLIAM from St. Helena who being in the service of the Hon. East India Company who with great economy and industry for 19 years honourably discharged his duty with great satisfaction to his employers and in the 49th year of his age departed this life in peace and with peace with all men on the 24th day January 1807 and is buried in Walton Churchyard.   Also ISABEL YOUNG their daughter died at Crossbankhead May 8th 1814 aged 75 years And ROBERT YOUNG son of the said John Young died New Langholm October 12th 1825 aged 75 years

55   Here lies WILLIAM YOUNG late tenant in Glindivin [sic] died January 17 1760 of age 55.   As also children died in infancy

56   In memory of JAMES EASTON died at Murrayfield 19th December 1846 aged 78 years   Also ISABELLA MURRAY his spouse died 10th September 1852 aged 75 years   Also MARGARET their daughter died at Meikledalehaugh 22nd August 1821 aged 6 years

57   In memory of WALTER ANDERSON who died at Burngrain 23rd March 1840 aged 77 years   Also MARGARET ELLIOT his spouse who died at Rigfoot 20th March 1842 aged 66 years Also MARGARET THOMSON wife of Walter Anderson their son who died at Sandyhaugh 7th March 1876 aged 59 years Also WALTER ANDERSON her husband who died at Kilmarnock 20th December 1888 aged 73 years

58 In memory of MICHAEL ANDERSON tenant Gorrindberry died
    30th April 1843 aged 84 years   Also CHRISTAN LAIDLOW
    spouse to the above Michael Anderson died at Gorrinberry 28th
    March 1831 aged 86 years   Also their children CHRISTAN
    died at the age of 2 and WILLIAM died in infancy

59 In memory of WILLIAM ANDISON died at Kirkstyle February
    28 1788 aged 73. JANET BLEAK his spouse February 1785
    aged – (no age cut) Likewise WILLIAM their son died in infancy

60 In memory of ELIZABETH ELLIOT wife of James Scott
    shepherd in Burnfoot Ewes 29th October 1843 aged 52 years
    MARY SCOTT their daughter April 1823 aged 4 years   Also
    ELIZABETH SCOTT their daughter died May 1839 aged 22
    years   Also the said JAMES SCOTT died at Dryden,
    Teviothead 25th May 1875 aged 80 years (post 1855 inscriptions,
    but memorial not found)

61 Here lye JOHN ARMSTRONG of Sorbie who died March 17th
    1685 aged 53 MARGARET MURRAY his spouse who died May
    17th 1716 aged 76 years And JOHN ARMSTRONG their son
    who died November 6th 1698 aged 14 years "Whither thou be
    old or young think upon the time to come"

62 Here lyes JOHN TELFER herd in Billhope 20 February 1760 53
    years And MARGARET ELLIOT his spouse 5 March 1779 (no
    age cut)

63 In memory of ANDREW LAMB died at Kirkstile July 6, 1758
    aged 44 years

64 In memory of ELIZABETH HUTTON daughter of John Hutton
    Glendivin died at Kirkstile 24th July 1844 aged 46 years

65 In memory of JOHN HUTTON who died in Hawick 1st January
    1864 aged 45 years and is interred there   Also ANN VICKERS

his wife who died at Bogfoot 18th May 1843 aged 26 years
Also GRACE their daughter who died 3rd December 1865 aged
23 years

66 In memory of ALEXANDER HUTTON died in Drummondshall
June 1829 aged 38 years And WILLIAM his son died in
infancy   Also a second WILLIAM his son who died 7th
July 1830 aged 16 years   Also ELIZABETH his daughter
who died at Bogfoot 27th March 1869 aged 43 years   Also
ANN IRVING his relict wife of William Welsh who died at
Bogfoot 14th March 1881 aged 87 years   Also the said
WILLIAM WELSH who died at Bogfoot 24th November 1885
aged 77 years

67 Here lyes DAVID LITTLE in Langholm died August 11, 1737
aged – years   Also JEAN LITTLE his spouse September 24,
1728 aged – years Their son SIMON LITTLE in Nityholm
December 30, 1765 aged 56 ISOBEL THOMSON his spouse
November 12, 1756 aged 46 Several of their children

68 Here lyes THOMAS LITTLE son to the Laird of Mickledale an
honest gentleman and well beloved by all the country who dyed
in April 27th 1665 his age 67. Here lyes SIMON LITTLE in Wrea
son to the aforesaid Thomas Little who departed this life 23rd
January 1716 aged 77.   Also SIMON LITTLE in Terrona
son to the above Simon Little in Wrea died February 8, 1757
aged 72 years   Also MARGARET his spouse died 8th March
1787, 88. Here also lyes interred JAMES LITTLE in Terrona who
departed this life April 7, 1799 aged 58 years   And JEAN his
spouse of Pious Memory died March 1, 1808 aged 74 years And
MARGARET their daughter who departed this life September
26, 1793 aged 21 years Likewise their children JOHN and JANET
died in infancy In memory of ARCHIBALD LITTLE in Terrona
died in Langholm 14th August 1850 aged 76 years Erected to the
memory of SIMON LITTLE tenant in Terrona who died
September 1757 aged 72 years

69 THOMAS ARMSTRONG died in New Langholm May 5, 1805 aged 74 years And JANET LAIDLAW his spouse died 2nd April 1769 aged 31 years   Also WILLIAM their son died at Antigua aged 28 years   Also THOMAS their son died in infancy and HELEN their daughter died at New Langholm 4th April 1847 aged 79 years

70 (Reverse of 69) In memory of WILLIAM ARMSTRONG shepherd in Mosspeeble September 28, 1782 aged 55 years

71 THOMAS ARMSTRONG interred here died December 1757 66 years. Here lies HELLEN IRVING spouse to Thomas Armstrong tenant in Over Fedling died March 28, 1750 52 years Several of his children

72 Erected in memory of GEORGE RUTHERFORD shepherd in Lodgegill who died 21st June 1853 aged 69 years   Also MARY JACKSON his relict who died at Lodgegill May 16th 1854 aged 58 years   Also GEORGE their son who died at Catcleugh, North Tyne March 17th 1840 aged 23 years   Also WALTER their son who died at Lodgegill 14th December 1840 aged 21 years   Also MARY their daughter who died at Lodgegill 31st March 1852 aged 21 years   Also MARGARET their daughter wife of James Rutherford who died in Langholm 1st December 1878 aged 33 years   Also THOMAS RUTHERFORD their son who died at Melrose 28th September 1911 aged 84 years

73 To the memory of SIMON JACKSON shepherd died at Dorniegill September 18, 1855 aged 61 years   Also MARY JARDINE wife of Simon Jackson, shepherd in Dorniegill died 25th March 1853 aged 55 years   Also JAMES their son died at Arkleton 26th April 1828 aged 7 years   Also WALTER their grandson who died June 1856 on board the Ship E.C. Scranton aged 11 years and was buried in Atlantic Ocean "The once loved form now cold and dead each mournful thought employs and nature

weeps her comforts fled, and withered all her joys. Then cease fond nature cease thy tears religion points on high the everlasting spring that appears and joys which can not die"

74   Here lyes JOHN JACKSON herd in Arklitoun Shiels died March 10 1780, 60. MARGRET TAIT his spouse died January 9, 1794, 63.

75   (Reverse of 74) In memory of JAMES JACKSON son to Simon Jackson, Arkleton died April 26th 1828 aged 7 years

76   In memory of JAMES JACKSON late shepherd at Arkleton died at Arkleton February 27th 1837 aged 80 years   Also ELSPETH ARMSTRONG spouse to James Jackson, Arkletonshiel died January 28th 1815 aged 60 years   Also WALTER their son died August 5th 1803 aged 12 years   Also MARGARET ARMSTRONG sister-in-law to James Jackson died at Sandyhaugh May 5, 1834 aged 68 years

77   Erected in memory to FRANCIS CHISHOLM tenant in Outer-woodhead died May 30th 1788 aged 88 years JANET ELLIOT his spouse died March 10th 1778 aged 52 years   Also FRANCIS their son died December 1771 aged – years and WILLIAM CHISHOLM late in Woodhead died at Langholm October 1816 aged 67 years   Also JANE SCOTT his spouse died at Langholm January __, 18__ aged _ years   Also WALTER BELL died at Langholm June 20th 1859 (?39) aged 39 (?59) years   Also MARY CHISHOLM his wife who died at Langholm 22nd October 1876 aged 78 years   Also WILLIAM CHISHOLM who died in LAngholm 4th October 1879 aged 76 years and JESSIE CHISHOLM who died in London 28th April 1875 aged 62 years

78   In memory of WILLIAM LITTLE _____ in Wrae who departed this life April 6, 1772 aged 84 years _____ to the late THOMAS LITTLE in Meikledale and HELEN GLENLSTEN spouse to William Little who died _____ (badly worn stone)

79 In memory of ISABELLA LITTLE daughter of Matthew Little and Mary Beattie who died at Broomholm 20th January 1846 in the second year of her age   Also the said MARY BEATTIE who died there 20th October 1856 aged 34 years   Also JAMES LITTLE their son who died 15th March 1865 aged 7 years   Also the above MATTHEW LITTLE who died at Langholm 2nd May 1883 aged 73 years   Also ISABELLA LITTLE who died at 11 Charlotte St. Langholm 24th December 1926 aged 80 years   Also GEORGE LITTLE who died at 11 Charlotte Street, Langholm 15th April 1932 in his 80th year

80 In memory of GEORGE LITTLE in Starnishwater died August 8, 1778 aged 85 years   Also his spouse MARGARET GRAHAM died April 1772 aged 72 years

81 In memory of WILLIAM LITTLE son to Simon Little in Stennishwater died 28th August 1768 aged 1 year   Also the said SIMON LITTLE died at Stennishwater 17th July 1797 aged 71 years   Also JANET GLENDINNING his spouse died March 29th 1811 aged 82 years   Also GEORGE their son died April 24th 1810 aged 51 years

82 (Reverse of 81) In memory of MARGARET LITTLE daughter of Simon Litttle died at Damhead 22nd January 1860 in the 90th year of her age

83 Here lyes THOMAS LITTLE tent in Carlisgill died January 4, 1720 aged 75 years   Also MARGARET GRAHAM his spouse died November 5, 1739 aged 76 years

84 In memory of HELEN daughter of John Anderson died at Wisp 13th November 1843 aged 14 months

85 In memory of JAMES HALL, Road Contractor, died at Flaskholm July 16th 1837 aged 46 years   Also JANET HALL died at Fiddleton January 25th 1859   Also JOHN HALL their son

died at Flaskholm May 5th 1825 aged 23 years   Also WILLIAM HALL their son died on passage home from Jamaica June 1829 aged 25 years   And ARCHIBALD HALL their son died at Flaskholm January 5th 1840 aged 31 years

86   In memory of JOHN ANDERSON, shepherd, who died at Breconridge 26th February 1838 aged 72 years   Also HELEN DICKSON spouse of John Anderson who died at Unthank April 13th 1834 aged 48 years CHARLES ANDERSON who died at Breconridge 25th November 1901 aged 85 years   Also JANE SMITH his wife who died 21st February 1912 aged 83 years   Also MARY their daughter who died 30th October 1911 aged 51 years   Also ROBERT ANDERSON who died 3rd September 1910 aged 65 years   Also AGNES SMITH ANDERSON their daughter who died 26th March 1922 aged 49 years   Also JOHN their son who died 26th January 1928 aged 59 years   Also ADAM their son who died 19th May 1928 aged 63 years

87   Here lyes the body of WILLIAM BEATY late in Bogg died in Hardensyd July 13, 1748 aged 67 years GRIZEL – his spouse (stone badly worn)

88   In memory of ELIZABETH HILL spouse to John Little, Tenant in Barrascrofts died April 1st 1832 aged 55 years   Also the said JOHN LITTLE 10th March 1853 aged 74 Children : JANE 31st October 1812 aged 6 years WILLIAM 31st October 1812 aged 6   JOHN died 21st July 1830 aged 8 years MARGARET ALLISON died July 24, 1830 aged 4 years JAMES died 8th July 1839 aged 20 years

89   Erected in memory of JOHN DALGLISH died at Winterhopehead 5th March 1774 aged 52 years   Also his daughter ISBEL died 1775 aged 2 years   Also JANNET LITTLE his wife died 21st June (no year cut) aged 80 years   Also JAMES died September 10th 1782 aged __ THOMAS died in Virgin (ia?) aged 26 years

90   Erected in memory of JOHN CHISHOLM tenant in Sheile in the Parish of Westerkirk February 12, 1741 age _4 years   Also MARGARET

ARMSTRONG his spouse died January 19, 1777 aged 88 years   Also THOMAS their son died December 15, 1745 ? aged 26 years   Also WILLIAM AND ROZIE their son and daughter died in infancy   Also of JOHN CHISHOLM their son tenant in Sheil died February 3, 1792 aged 62 years   Also MARGARET CHISHOLM died February 2nd 1802 aged 80 years   Also JEAN died January 10th 1810 aged 82 years – daughters of John Chisholm and Margaret Armstrong

91 In memory of ROBERT CHISHOLM died in Sheil 1758 aged 75 years   Also of ROBERT CHISHOLM tenant in Sheill son of John Chisholm and Margaret Armstrong died May 28th 1817 aged 85 years

92 Here lyes JOHN BELL in Glendiven February 20, 1746 aged 75 years And MARGARET _____ his spouse January 27, 1737 aged __ (badly worn stone)

93 In memory of JOHN HIGAMS (Higgans?) died in Monsrigg 1724 aged 45   MARGARET BELL his spouse died December 1741 aged 50 year

94 Here lyes THOMAS HOGG in Byrecleughwater September 26, 1738 aged 61.   Also HELEN LITTLE his spouse died July 13th 1758 aged 58 years   Also HELEN their daughter died November 7th (no year or age cut)

95 In memory of GEORGE SCOTT, shepherd in Lodgegill who died July 2nd 1823 aged 61 years   Also MARGARET MURRAY his spouse who died at Newcastleton April 21st 1846 aged 75 years   Also JANE their daughter died July 7th 1822 aged 22 years

96 (Reverse of 95) In memory of JOHN SCOTT son of Margaret Scott who died at Loganhead 5th March 1871 aged 4 years

97 DAVID ARMSTRONG who dyed in Terrona 1688

98 Here lyes WILLIAM MURRAY weaver in Terrona died in April 21, 1721 of age 58 and his spouse MARGRAT MOFFAT who died in January 15, 1721 of age 62

99 In memory of WILLIAM MURRAY weaver who died at Kirkstyle April 8th 1827 age 77 years   Also MARY THOMSON his spouse who died at Kirkstyle November 27th 1822 aged 72 years   Also JAMES MURRAY their son joiner who died there December 11, 1821 aged 25 years ANNE MURRAY their daughter who died at Howgill February 10th 1802 aged 14 years   Also ELIZABETH MURRAY their daughter who died at Drumlanrig Mains 19th October 1865 aged 74 years Buried in Penpont Churchyard

100 (Reverse of 99) In memory of ISABELLA wife of George Lethem joiner, Drumlanrig and daughter of William Murray she died 16th April 1845 aged 60 years. She left a husband and six children to lament her loss.   Also JANET their daughter who died 3rd April 1834 aged 20 years interred in Penpont Churchyard Also MARY their daughter who died 16th November 1854 aged 43 years   Also above GEORGE LETHEM who died 19th January 1862 aged 79 years

101 Here lyes MARGARET GRAHAM daughter to James Graham in Meikeldale who died November 14th 1728 of age 18 years

102 In memory of JEAN FLETCHER spouse to Thomas Murray who died in Linhope April 23rd 1806 aged 44 years   Also ISABEL their daughter who died October 1808 aged 16 years   Also ELIZABETH their daughter who died December 24th 1823 aged 2 years and 6 months   Also above THOMAS MURRAY who died at Rigghead December 19th 1827 aged 66 years

103 In memory of GEORGE MURRAY herd in Lodgegill who died May 5th 1814 aged 82 years   Also MARGARET RIDDELL his spouse who died February 27th 1825 aged 96 years   Also WALTER his son who died December 1774 aged 12 years   Also GIDEON his son who died January 7th 1814 aged 48 years

104 In memory of JANET CAIRNS spouse to George Murray herd in Billhope who died October 30th 1815 aged 42 years   Also THOMAS their son who died April 25th 1803 aged 6 months Also GEORGE their son who died November 29th 1807 aged 5 months   Also JOHN their son who died at Enzieholm September 12th 1823 aged 22 years

105 In memory of JOHN MURRAY Tenant in Bailliehill who died March 31st 1813 aged 67 years   Also ISABEL FAIRBAIRN spouse to John Murray in Bailliehill who died January 12th 1796 aged 32 years

106 In memory of MATTHEW MURRAY in Bentpath who died March 3rd 1787 aged 84 years   Also AGNES PURVES his spouse who died January 15th 1798 aged 91 years

107 (Reverse of 106) Here lyes JOHN son to Matthew Murray in Bentpath September 15th 1743 aged 3 years   Also THOMAS his son who died September 15th 1743 aged 7 months

108 Here lyes ROBERT EASTON in Ewislees son of William Easton there who died January 28th 1772 aged 37 years   Also AGNES MURRAY spous e to said William Easton who died at Burnfoot November 17th 1750 aged 31 years   Also JEAN their daughter who died April 3rd 1742 aged 5 years

109 Interred here the remains of WILLIAM EASTON in Hougill who died 15th October 1795 aged 47 years   Also ANN SMITH his spouse who died 7th June 1796 aged 50 years   Also their son ROBERT EASTON who died at Burnfoot, Westerkirk 2nd

May 1851 aged 71 years   Also MARGARET SCOTT his relict who died there 18th January 1858 aged 72 years   Also two children who died in infancy   And ROBERT EASTON their son who died at Burnfoot 7th May 1873 aged 51 years   Also HELEN WRIGHT his wife who died at Burnfoot 15th February 1871 aged 44 years "And they shall see His face"

110   (Reverse of 109) ROBERT THOMSON grandson of Robert Easton who died at Burnfoot 1st August 1853 aged 23 years

111   In memory of JANET BROUN spouse to William Easton in Ewislees who died 11th March 1775 aged 63 years   Also said WILLIAM EASTON in Howgill who died 8th November 1787 aged 83 years   Also THOMAS EASTON their son who died in Kirkpatrick 17th May 1781 aged 27 years   Also JAMES EASTON their son who died in Langholm February 14th 1804 aged 79 years

112   In memory of DAVID MURRAY tenant in Whisgills who died October 6th 1776 aged 72 years   Also ELIZABETH MURRAY his spouse who died April 11th 1791 aged 75 years   Also AGNESS their daughter who died April 7th 1746 aged 6 years   Also WILLIAM EASTON their son who died February 6th 1760 aged 1 year   Also DAVID who died June 15th 1758 aged 15 years

113   Here lyes JAMES EASTON son of John Easton in Hawick who died at Burnfoot (no dates) Erected by his uncle William Easton

114   In memory of MATTHEW MURRAY who died at Minsca 23rd May 1849 aged 79 years   Also JANE GRAHAM spouse of Matthew Murray who died at Allfornought 20th October 1845 aged 77 years   Also ISABELLA their daughter who died 8th December 1848 aged 55 years   Also MATTHEW their son who died at Minsca 11th June 1849 aged 37 years

115 (Reverse of 114) In memory of DAVID MURRAY he died at Barclose-head 19th July 1789 aged 52 years   Also SARAH TELFORD his spouse who died at Kerr September 27th 1824 aged 77 years And his children JOHN who died at Conhess 16th April 1770 age 1 year   Also THOMAS who died at Barclosehead 26th July 1789 age 5 weeks   Also SARAH MURRAY their daughter died at Wattaman December 19th 1811 aged 32 years

116 To the memory of the undermentioned family late in Hopsrigg ARCHIBALD SCOTT who died 22nd of January 1768 aged 86 years   Also MARGARET CRANSTON his spouse who died 30th of June 1758 aged 61 years   Also THOMAS SCOTT their oldest son who died 25th July 1758 aged 41 years Also JOHN SCOTT son of aforesaid Archibald who died 4th February 1795 aged 68 years   Also JANET GRAHAM his spouse who died 31st May 1779 aged 47 years

117 To the memory of JAMES SCOTT in Fingland son of Archibald Scott in Hopsrigg who died 1st November 1764 aged 35 years Likewise in memory of his son JAMES SCOTT who died at Enzieholm 7th June 1805 aged 39 years   Also MARGARET his daughter age 2 years and WILLIAM his son nine years (no dates)   Also JAMES his son who died at Enzieholm 16th June 1821 aged 23 years   Also MARY BEATTIE his spouse who died at Watcarrick 10th January 1846 aged 74 years

118 In memory of JOHN SCOTT, Tenant in Enzieholm, son to the late Captain James Scott who died 11th May 1838 aged 36 years   Also of MARGARET BROWN wife of said John Scott who died 7th March 1874 aged 69 years

119 In memory of ROBERT SCOTT Eweslees who died 6th November 1868 aged 72 years   Also VIOLET SCOTT his wife who died 28th March 1870 aged 63 years (fallen memorial deeply embedded)

120 In memory of BEATRIX LAMB died at Kirkandrews March 1814 aged 18 years   Also WILLIAM LAMB her brother who died at Woodhead October 17, 1820 aged 22 years Also THOMAS LAMB their father tenant in New Woodhead who died there June 29, 1826 aged 74 years   Also THOMAS LAMB his son late in New Woodhead died there January 11, 1835 aged 34 years Also JANE AITCHISON his spouse who died at Todhillwood 1st August 1843 aged 83 years

121 In memory of MARY JOHNSTON daughter of William Johnston who died at Campknows February the 25th 1844 aged 18 years   Also WILLIAM their son who died 5th September 1857 aged 37 years   Also the said WILLIAM JOHNSTON who died 3rd December 1865 aged 76 years   Also ISABELLA LITHGOW his wife who died at Langholm 26th July 1885 aged 92 years

122 In memory of JOHN TELFORD who died at Ellerbeck who died 8th October 1823 aged 65 years   Also JANET ARMSTRONG his spouse who died at Newcastleton December 28th 1846 aged 75 years   Also MARY their daughter who died at Barnglieshhead May 25th 1824 aged 22 years   Also WILLIAM their son who died at Maidestone [*sic*] County of Kent, September 5th 1831 aged 25 years (post 1855 inscriptions – memorial not found)

123 In memory of JAMES TELFER tenant in Potholm who died December 5th 1800 aged 75 years   Also MARGARET IRVING spouse to James Telfer, tenant in Potholm, who died August 21st 1790 aged 57 years   Also DAVID TELFER their son late tenant in Potholm who died at Langholm January 25th 1835 aged 78 years

124 Here lyes JEAN TELFER spouse to David Murray in Burnfoot who died October 12 day 1728 of age 56 years

125 Here lyes JOHN ELLIOT in Glendivin who died May 23 day 1699 aged 82 years   Also his spouse HELEN McVITIE who died the 23 day 16— of age 38 years

126 In memory of ADAM OGILVIE fourth son of John Laurie and Ann Grieve a Lieutenant of Royal Marines who died at sea A.D. 1814 aged 20 years and 6 months   Also WILLIAM LAURIE their second son Brevit [*sic*] Major and Captain of Royal Marines who died at Chatham 1842 aged 54 years

127 (continued on another side) Here lies the mortal remains of ROBERT fifth son of John Laurie and Anne Grieve who died at Langholm A.D. 1828 aged 30½ years   Also MAJOR GENERAL JOHN LAURIE their third son who died at Landulas, North Wales 20th July 1861 aged 69 years   Also of their youngest son WALTER LAURIE surgeon 4th Regt. Madras Light Cavalry who died of cholera 24th April 1844 at Annantepit in India aged 59 years

128 (continued on another side) Here lie the mortal remains of the REVEREND JOHN LAURIE Minister of the Parish of Ewes who died at the Manse A.D. 1817 aged 72 years   Also ANNE GRIEVE wife of the Reverend John Laurie who died at Langholm A.D. 1834 aged 73 years   Also of JAMES LAURIE their eldest son, Lieutenant in the Royal Marines who died at Georgefield 17th June 1851 aged 64 years (see notes)

129 (continued on another side) Here lie the mortal remains of MARY eldest daughter of John Laurie and Anne Grieve who died at the Manse A.D. 1794 aged 4½ years   Also of MARY sister of John Laurie who died at Ewes Manse A.D. 1804 age (uncut)

130 In memory of MARGARET WYLIE daughter of Andrew Wylie who died at Unthank, May the 24th 1843 aged 12 years   Also JOHN WYLIE their son who died September the 28th 1855 aged 31 years   Also WILHELMINA ARMSTRONG spouse of

Andrew Wylie who died 17th October 1865 aged 78 years
Also the said ANDREW WYLIE who died at Campknows 2nd
January 1868 aged 70 years   Also JOHN WILSON their
son-in-law who died at Roadend Tollbar 20th June 1874 aged 52
years "From his lips there came not a murmur in the depth of his
sickness and pain he would live a bit longer for Jesus yet to die
and be with Him is gain"

131 Here lyes MARGRET LAINGE [sic] spouse to James Gladstans
[sic] in Kirkstyle who died on the 5 day of March 1721 of age 65
years

132 In memory of JOHN LITTLE late in Kirtonburnside who died
April 18, 1792 aged 91 years and of ELIZABETH RICHARDSON
his spouse who died December 16, 1791 aged 73 years   Also
GEORGE LITTLE their son late surgeon in Langholm who
died April 29, 1789 aged 40 and ELIZABETH LITTLE their
daughter who died September __ 1772 (remainder illegible-badly
worn)

133 In memory of WILLIAM IRVING, farmer in Glendivan who died
22nd March 1851 aged 86 years   Also HENRIETTA IRVING
his spouse who died 16th October 1859 aged 73 years   Also
JOHN IRVING his son who died 26th February 1854 aged
42 years   Also JANET IRVING his daughter who died 5th
August 1854 aged 37 years   Also ARCHIBALD IRVING his
son who died 10th August 1884 aged 71 years   Also ROBERT
IRVING his son who died at Pingle Bridge 1st April 1891 aged
64 years Also ISABELLA IRVING his daughter who died at Pingle
10th April 1895 aged 80 years (in-scribed on reverse) In memory
of AGNES IRVING spouse of Walter Byers who died at
Newcastleton 24th January 1860 aged 52 years

134 In memory of ROBERT ELLIOT son to John Elliot in Coombes
who died September 30th 1782 aged 72 years   Also his son
ROBERT ELLIOT who died February 1771 age 11 years

135 Erected to the memory of GEORGE PATERSON son of James Paterson in Wrae and Margaret Brand who died in Edinburgh 28th January 1834 aged 16 years and whose remains be interred here   Also said MARGARET BRAND who died at Terrona 30th October 1859 aged 69 years   Also said JAMES PATERSON who died at Terrona 10th December 1876 aged 86 years (post 1855 inscriptions – memorial not found)

136 To the memory of ALEXANDER POTT who died at Burnfoot, Ewes 9th October 1859 aged 66 years   Also APALINA HOGARTH his wife who died 2nd November 1836 aged 40 years Also APALINA HOGARTH their daughter who died 4th July 1828 aged 1 year and 5 months "I am the resurrection and the life"

137 In memory of WALTER BORTHWICK in Hopesrig who died 10th January 1807 aged 96 years   Also HELEN his daughter and JEAN   Also of THOMAS CHALMERS BORTHWICK, Tenant in Hopsrigg and Langshawburn who died in Milnholm 16th December 1888 in his 76th year and of his wife MARGARET CURLL SCOTT eldest daughter of the late Alexander John Scott, Esq., of Knockhill who died at 33 St. Bernards Cres. Edinburgh, 8th June 1883 in her 71st year and was interred here

138 In memory of JANET BORTHWICK relict of the late John Little, Esq., Chaple, who died in Langholm 14th November 1855 aged 83 years

139 In memory of WALTER BORTHWICK in Hopsrig who died 11th October 1812 aged 33 years THOMAS died at Sorbie 1790 aged 17 years JOHN, late Capt. H.M. 12th Regiment of Foot who died at Rosevale, Langholm in May 1837 aged 49 years JANE died at Langholm 20th April 1871 aged 87 years and of their parents   WILLIAM only son of Thomas Borthwick in Sorbie and Jean Elliot his wife, who died in Edinburgh in August 1792 aged 42 years and was buried in Grey Friars Churchyard there.

ELIZABETH HAY his wife, only child of Alexdr. Hay, Portioner of Inveresk died at Langholm February 1833 aged 83 years and was interred here.

140   In memory of ROBERT WAUGH who died at Fiddleton Bar 29th September 1853 in the 67th year of his age   Also MARY IRVING wife of the above who died at Fiddleton Cottage 11th July 1897 aged 80 years

141   In memory of THOMAS BORTHWICK tenant in Sorbie who died in December 1793 aged 83 years and his spouse JEAN ELLIOT daughter of William Elliot Esq. of Borthwick Brae who died in August 1792 aged 76 years   WALTER BORTHWICK who died 23rd December 1825 aged 10 years third son of Alexdr. Hay Borthwick in Hopsrig   Also ISABELLA his daughter who died 19th August 1827 aged 19 years   Also ELIZABETH BORTHWICK his daughter who died at Hopsrig on the 1st July 1834 aged 25 years   Also the above ALEXANDER HAY BORTHWICK, Tenant in Hopsrig son of William Borthwick and Elizabeth Hay who died 16th February 1837 in his 60th year and of AGNES CHALMERS his wife who died in Georgefield on the 7th day of August 1860 aged 81 years. Erected by Elizabeth Hay

142   In memory of JOHN ANDERSON who died in Flaskholmhead November 10th 1806 aged 69 years and AGNES RAE his spouse who died in 1824 aged 82 years   Also ROBERT ANDERSON their son who died at Wrae 3rd June 1870 aged 92 years   Also SARAH NICOL spouse to Robert Anderson, Shepherd at Linhope, who died September 16th 1843 aged 66 years   Also WALTER aged 28 ROBERT 24   ARCHIBALD 10 and AGNES 41 (14?) children of the above Robert Anderson and Sarah Nicol all interred here

143   In memory of THOMAS SINCLAIR, Shoemaker in Langholm who died 1st July 1851 aged 32 years Erected by his wife Mary Sword

144 In memory of JOHN SWORD, joiner son of James Sword and Helen Brown who died at Brieryshaw 22nd April 1843 aged 28 years   Also ISABEL who died in infancy

145 In memory of MATTHEW WELSH who died at Sandyhaugh on the 6th day of January 1849 aged 54 years   Also MARGARET LAIDLAW his wife who died at Sandyhaugh on the 9th of October 1886 aged 90 years   Also two of his children who died in infancy   Also MARGARET his daughter who died 9th June 1869 aged 39 years   Also MARGARET DODDS his mother-in-law who died at Sandyhaugh 6th July 1839 aged 73 years

146 In memory of WILLIAM WELSH who died at Kirkstyle who died April 22nd 1853 aged 80 years   Also HELEN BEATTIE his spouse who died November 27th 1847 aged 85 years ANN WELSH who died 28th July 1825 aged 34 years and JANE who died in infancy   Also JANE WELSH their daughter who died at Kirkstyle January 11th 1891 aged 87 years

147 Here lyes WILHEMINA MURRAY daughter to Charles Murray tenant in Broomholm who died March 1750

148 In memory of JOHN GLENDINNING who died in Meickledale-haugh 7th November 1787 aged 70 years   Also his spouse EUPHAM GLENDINNING who died 23rd April 1798 aged 69 years

149 In memory of ROBERT BAPTIE who died at Mospeble who died May 20th 1796 aged 30 years

150 In memory of THOMAS ARMSTRONG in New Langholm who died April 19th 1801 aged 86 years   Also his spouse JANET NICOL who died February 13th 1813 aged 87 years   Also ROBERT son to Thomas Armstrong, Crossbank who died July 19th 1772 aged 2 years and 6 months   Also MARGARET his daughter who died at Irvine, November 18th 1789 aged 34

years   Also ANDREW his son who died July 3rd 1799 aged
33 years

151   (Reverse of 150) In memory of JOHN ARMSTRONG, shoemaker
        who died 28th March 1858 aged 72 years

152   Here lyes CATHERINE of unspotted fame spouse to Adam
        Dryden smith in Kirkstile who died May 31, 1732 of age 36 years

153   In memory of ROBERT BYERS who died at Fiddleton Tollbar
        22nd July 1855 aged 79 years   Also HELEN CLARK his relict
        who died at Billmansknowe 19th September 1861 aged 76
        years   Also of ROBERT son of Robert Byers he died in infancy
        at Howgill on the 3rd April 1813   Also JANET his daughter
        who died at Gillesbie Tollhouse 3rd September 1846 aged 24
        years   Also ROBERT T. MUIR his grandson who died at Dinley
        5th September 1849 aged 7 years   Also MARGARET BYERS
        daughter of Robert Byers who died at 13 Drumlanrig Square,
        Hawick 23rd June 1910 aged 86 years

154   In memory of WILLIAM BYERS who died at Cleuchhead 1st
        August 1866 aged 55 years   Also JANET KELLY his spouse
        who died at Dinlee [sic] April 12th 1845 aged 31 years   Also
        JANET KETCHIN his wife who died at Hawick 16th December
        1891 aged 72 years

155   In memory of the REVEREND ROBERT SHAW, Minister of this
        Parish who died 16th April 1853 in the 73rd year of his age and
        47th of his ministry and MARY MONCRIEFF his spouse who
        died 9th July 1856 aged 62 years   Also WILLIAM their son
        who died 15th January 1831 aged 3 years   Also MARGARET
        their daughter who died 27th February 1843 aged 17 years and
        ANNE JANET their daughter who died at Hexham 25th June
        1864 aged 34 years   Also GEORGE their eldest son who died
        at Hawick 10th December 1885 aged 66 years   Also JANE
        their daughter who died at Archbank, Moffat 23rd June 1889

aged 68 years   Also HELEN MARY their youngest daughter who died at Highfield, Holmer, Hereford 16th August 1906 aged 67 years   Also MARION MONCRIEFF their last surviving daughter who died at Edinburgh 15th July 1923 aged 88 years (See Notes)

156   GEORGE ARMSTRONG his son who died January 21, 1777 age 25 years (stone fragment)

157   Erected to the memory of GIDEON SCOTT son of Robert Scott Esq. Todshawhaugh late tenant in Middlemoss who died at Broomholmknowe June 14th 1834 aged 38 years Also BARBARA ARMSTRONG wife of the above who died at Eweslees 30th May 1860 aged 80 years

158   Sacred to the memory of HELEN beloved wife of John W. Common who died at Meikledale October 7th 1934 aged 29 years   Also the above JOHN WILLIAM COMMON who died at Innerfield, Lochmaben, November 11th 1947 aged 46 years

159   Sacred to the memory of MARGARET ANNE DOUGLAS died at Arkleton Farm May 17th 1931 aged 34 years   Also of JANE MURRAY wife of John Douglas and mother of the above died at Longwood Lodge January 26th 1948 aged 70 years (post 1950 ins)

160   Sacred to the memory of WILLIAM BEATTIE eldest son of Thomas and Jean B. Scott who died at Hoghill 27th April 1931 aged 36 years   Also the above JANE B. SCOTT who died at Hoghill 23rd September 1932 aged 67 years   Also the above THOMAS SCOTT Farmer who died at Hoghill 23rd November 1939 aged 66 years (post 1950 ins)

161   In loving memory of BARBARA SCOTT wife of John Grieve who died at Eweslees 11th February 1918 aged 89 years   Also

the above JOHN GRIEVE Farmer, Eweslees who died 25th March 1921 aged 84 years

162   In memory of RICHARD COMMON who died at Meikledale 4th November 1939 aged 84 years   Also his wife JANE DOUGLAS who died at Meikledale 13th January 1943 aged 73 years

163   In loving memory of JAMES DOUGLAS ELLIOT son of Andrew and Margaret Elliot who died at Mosspeeble 1st August 1915 aged 2 years and 8 months   Also the above ANDREW ELLIOT of Eweslees and Tenant in Mosspeeble who died there 28th June 1931 aged 48 years   Also the above MARGARET DOUGLAS HENDERSON who died at Mosspeeble 27th March 1942 aged 56 years

164   In memory of ANDREW SCOTT THOMSON, Farmer, beloved husband of Elliot Armstrong who died at Blackhall 11th January 1915 aged 62 years   Also the above ELLIOT ARMSTRONG who died at Glenvorn January 18th 1928 aged 70 years

165   In memorium JESSIE ELLIOT ELLIOT wife of James Church Little, Burnfoot, Ewes who died 6th April 1906 aged 44 years Also the above JAMES CHURCH LITTLE died 15th February 1912 aged 65 years

166   In memory of JANET AITCHISON wife of James Douglas Elliot who died at Mosspeeble 20th April 1904 aged 59 years   Also the above JAMES DOUGLAS ELLIOT who died at Mosspeeble 20th June 1920 aged 80 years

167   In memory of ISABELLA SUSAN SCOTT THOMPSON wife of Matthew Welsh who died at Sandyhaugh 10th May 1902 aged 44 years   Also of the above MATTHEW WELSH who died at Park House, Broxburn 13th February 1926 aged 96 years

168 In memorium WILLIAM PATERSON of Holmfoot, Langholm died 17th October 1902 aged 77 years and of JANET ELLIOT his wife died at Holmfoot, Langholm, 18th May 1905 aged 72 years

169 In memorium JANE HUTCHISON SMITH eldest daughter of Robert Smith, Ladyland, born 20th September 1843 died 26th November 1912 THOMAS SMITH his eldest son who died at Eskbank, Langholm 7th June 1918 aged 77 years   Also AGNES GRIEG third daughter of the late Robert Smith, Ladyland Kirkbean, born at Ladyland 9th February 1854 died at Eskbank, Langholm 17th March 1929 (On base of memorial is the inscription) Father, Mother and Brother buried at Kirkbean

170 In memorium JOHN W.J.M. PATERSON born 27th February 1827 died 27th December 1904 MARION SMITH his wife born 21st January 1845 died at Eskbank 10th January 1923 ROBERT SMITH PATERSON born 8th January 1885 died 24th April 1901 (post 1950 inscription)

171 In memory of ALEXANDER WELSH PATERSON who died at Bush 1st July 1900 aged 71 years and CATHERINE M. PALMER his wife who died 4th January 1901 aged 52 years

172 In memory of JAMES MOFFAT who died at Broomholmshiels, Langholm 6th March 1916 aged 61 years   Also JANET ANDERSON his wife who died at Tarras Cottages, Langholm 22nd June 1918 aged 63 years MARGARET MOFFAT daughter of James Moffat who died at Sorbie Cottage, Ewes 30th August 1900 aged 27 years   Also JOHN MOFFAT son of James Moffat and Janet Anderson who died at the Hope Hospital, Langholm 9th October 1908 aged 12 years and 7 months Also THOMAS MOFFAT their second son and husband of Emily Bewley who died at the Hope Hospital, Langholm 14th October 1912 aged 31 years   Also Pte. ROBERT MOFFAT 11th Border Regiment their third son who was killed in action in France

1st July 1916 aged 28 years   Also WILLIAM MOFFAT their
eldest son who died at Broomholmshiels, Langholm 18th
November 1916 aged 38 years interred in North Merchiston
Cemetery, Edinburgh

173   In memory of JOHN JARDINE of Thorlieshope who died at
Arkleton, Ewes 30th March 1882 aged 70 years

174   In memory of JAMES DICKSON, Gardener, Castlemilk who died
there 17th April 1889 HELEN WELSH his widow who died at
Edinburgh 7th April 1906 GEORGE DICKSON, MD. OM. their
son who died at Edinburgh 3rd June 1923

175   In loving memory FRANCIS BLACKLOCK Arkleton Farm died
in the Hope Hospital, Langholm 19th June 1925 aged 63 years
Also ELIZABETH TELFER his wife died at St. Andrews 9th
December 1935 aged 76 years   Also his third son DAVID J.
T. BLACKLOCK Pte. 1/5 KOSB who died 24th May 1917 from
wounds received in action aged 21 years and FRANCIS who died
in infancy

176   In memory of WILLIAM and AGNES EWART Twin children of
William Ewart and Wilhelmina Harkness who died at Brieryshaw,
Ewes 18th May 1878 aged 16 days   Also ELIZABETH their
daughter who died 27th April 1883 aged 18 days   Also the
above WILHELMINA HARKNESS who died 27th November
1911 aged 66 years   Also the above WILLIAM EWART who
died 25th December 1912 aged 69 years

177   MARGARET STIRLING died at Ewes Schoolhouse 28th
February 1873 aged 61 years Erected by her daughter Helen Lyall
HELEN STIRLING wife of J. G. Lyall died 12th September 1878
aged 46 years

178   In memory of JOSEPH CLARK LYALL for 46 years Schoolmaster
of the Parish of Ewes born 9th October 1833 died 7th June 1913

and of his son WILLIAM JAMES LYALL, OBE. Lt.Col. Royal Engineers who died Nowshera Military Hospital, 29th November 1938 aged 52 years from injuries received in motor accident and is interred in Takaballa Cemetery, Peshawar and   Also of his wife JANET McCULLOCH Sandyhaugh, Ewes who died 1st August 1947 aged 88 years (post 1950 inscriptions)

179   CHARLES J LYALL who died at Ewes Schoolhouse 24th May 1893 aged 5 years

180   In memory of WILLIAM ARMSTRONG, Shepherd, Sorbie who died at Tumore, Sutherlandshire 15th June 1869 aged 34 years Also HELEN ROBINSON his wife who died at Langholm 20 December 1893 aged 58 years At rest (post 1950 inscription)

181   In memory of MARY ELLIOT spouse of John Common, Farmer, Meikledale who died 14th July 1860 aged 38 years JANET ELLIOT their daughter died 5th March 1858 aged 3 months and is interred in Unthank Churchyard reinterred here ELIZABETH ELLIOT their daughter died 23rd February 1865 aged 13 years Also the above JOHN COMMON who died 1st November 1888 aged 86 years and of AGNES MILLAR second wife of the said John Common who died 2nd April 1901 aged 82 years

182   In memory of ANDREW THOMSON Road Surveyor who died at Brieryshaw on the 25th May 1859 aged 75 years Inscribed quotation "Mark the perfect man, and behold the upright for the end of that man is peace." Psalm XXXVII v37 (sandstone memorial badly eroded)

183   In memory of ANN SHORTREED MONCRIEFF daughter of the Rev. W.H. Moncrieff Minister of Annan who died at Hawick January 8th 1877 aged 90 years

184   Sacred to the memory of MARGARET F. SUTHERLAND wife of the Rev. Thomas Smith who died 10th February 1869 aged 35

years   Also of the REV. THOMAS SMITH who died 2nd March 1901 aged 73 years in the 48th year of his ministry in the Parish of Ewes   Also RACHEL SUTHERLAND sister of the above who died 18th June 1916

185   In memory of ANDREW BYERS Shepherd, who died at Raeburn, Eskdalemuir 10th January 1893 aged 86 years   Also MARGARET MOFFAT his wife who died at Raeburn Eskdalemuir 16th March 1895 aged 82 years

186   In memory of JOHN BELL who died at Wrae 2nd July 1856 aged 31 years   Also JANET CAMPBELL his wife who died at Langholm 11th April 1911 aged 86 years   Also JANET BELL their daughter who died at Langholm 18th January 1913 aged 65 years   Also MARGARET BELL their daughter who died 22nd June 1926 aged 79 years interred at Brompton Cemetery, Chelsea   Also ANNIE BELL their daughter who died at Langholm 6th November 1927 aged 82 years   Also CHRISTINA CAMPBELL BELL who died 5th September 1944 aged 89 years

187   In memory of THOMAS BELL who died at Wrae April 24th 1857 aged 26 years   Also JANET BELL wife of the above who died at Heathfield, Lockerbie 8th March 1916 aged 89 years

188   In memory of AGNES ARMSTRONG wife of Andrew Bell who died at Wrae 3rd December 1862 aged 74 years   Also the above ANDREW BELL who died 19th September 1884 aged 85 years   Also JANET their daughter who died 9th April 1892 aged 65 years   Also MARGARET their daughter who died at Langholm 24th November 1905 aged 76 years

189   Sacred to the memory of JOHN PRINGLE, Shepherd who died at Blackhall 15th March 1869 aged 46 years   Also MARGARET SCOTT his wife who died at 5 St. Cuthbert's Terr. Hexham 22nd April 1902 aged 79 years

190 In memory of WILLIAM IRVING Shepherd who died at Bogfoot 11th July 1867 aged 42 years   Also ISABELLA SCOTT his wife who died in Langholm 28th July 1917 aged 91 years Also of their children ISABELLA MARY who died at Bogfoot, 27th May 1865 aged 14 days HENRIETTA who died at Bogfoot 27th December 1866 aged 19 months   Also WILLIAM their son who died Bellmyre, Illinois, North America 12th March 1870 aged 21 years   Also FRANK their son who died at Langholm 20th May 1920 aged 58 years   Also ARCHIBALD their son who died at Langholm 22nd July 1938 aged 82 years

191 In memory of WILLIAM ARMSTRONG who died at Geilfoot, Liddesdale 25th April 1866 aged 54 years   Also JANE IRVING his wife who died at Glendivan 20th June 1880 aged 71 years

192 In memory of JANE McVITTIE daughter of Alexander McVittie and Elizabeth Elliot who died at Flaskholm 14th January 1875 aged 18 years   Also the said ALEXANDER McVITTIE who died 20th July 1877 aged 58 years   Also ELIZABETH ELLIOT wife of the above Alexander McVittie who died 10th January 1900 aged 82 years   Also JOHN McVITTIE their son and beloved husband of Janet Moffat who died Cleughfoot, Hawick 4th March 1910 aged 50 years   Also the above JANET MOFFAT who died at Langholm 3rd March 1928 aged 63 years

193 In memory of JOHN McVITTIE who died in Langholm 23rd November 1867 aged 54 years Also JANE THOMPSON his wife who died 15th September 1865 aged 60 years   Also JANE their daughter who died 8th March 1899 aged 56 years   Also THOMAS E. McVITTIE who died 12th February 1921 aged 60 years (post 1950 inscription)

194 In memory of WILLIAM ELPHINSTONE MALCOLM of Burnfoot, Westerkirk born 27th December 1817 died 30th December 1907 aged 90 years

195   Erected in memory of JOHN LOCKIE who died at Hopsrigg 9th
      December 1839 aged 72 years   Also JANET his daughter who
      died in infancy

196   Sacred to the memory of MATILDA LOUISA widow of William
      Scott Elliot of Arkleton, born March 21st 1859 died August 4th
      1929 "She loved much"

197   Sacred to the memory of WILLIAM SCOTT ELLIOT of Arkleton
      born March 24th 1849 died September 2nd 1919 "Blessed are the
      pure in heart for they shall see God. Love is enough"

198   MARGARET wife of William Scott Elliot of Arkleton born 10th
      December 1824 died 16th March 1911 "He giveth his beloved sleep"

199   WILLIAM SCOTT ELLIOT of Arkleton born 22nd March 1811
      died 20th May 1901 "By grace are ye saved through faith it is the
      gift of God"

200   LOUISA ISOBEL SCOTT ELLIOT born September 22nd 1850
      died August 13th 1937 "There remaineth therefore a rest to the
      people of God"

201   MARY SCOTT ELLIOT born 28th October 1862 died 5th June
      1922 MARGARET SCOTT ELLIOT born 27th December 1855
      died 5th April 1925 "Blessed are the pure in heart for they shall
      see God. Blessed are they that mourn for they shall be comforted"

202   COLONEL ADAM SCOTT ELLIOT Queens Own Cameron
      Highlanders born 28th February 1860 died 12th December 1921
      and his wife MARGARET PIRIE ADAM born 1868 died 1951
      "So loved so mourned"

203   LOUIS ALEXANDER SCOTT ELLIOT born March 3rd 1858
      died October 2nd 1916 "A soul tempered fervant heroic and good
      helper and friend of mankind"

204 In memory of JANET JACKSON who died at Kirkstyle 16th June 1873 aged 85 years   Also MARGARET JACKSON who died in Langholm 5th October 1873 aged 82 years

205 In memory of JANET SLACK wife of Adam Ogilvie, Tenant in Cooms, who died at Cronksbank the 20th day of June 1878 aged 29 years   Also the above ADAM OGILVIE who died at Cooms 26th April 1890 aged 54 years

206 In memory of ROBERT ANDERSON who died at Cooms 9th July 1879 aged 23 years   Also SYBELLA OGILVIE his wife who died 8th September 1915 aged 75 years

207 In memory of MICHAEL McVITTIE Road Surveyor who died at Glendiven 7th September 1896 aged 89 years   Also JANE SCOTT his wife who died at Bogfoot 1st July 1905 aged 66 years   Also ROBERT their son who died in infancy

208 In memory of MAGGIE ELLIOT daughter of Thomas Elliot and Elizabeth Armstrong who died at Langholm 20th June 1886 aged 20 years   Also the above THOMAS ELLIOT who died at Langholm 28th February 1889 aged 62 years   Also the above ELIZABETH ARMSTRONG his wife who died at Glendivan 26th August 1919 in her 100th year (post 1950 inscription)

209 In memory of ANN ELLIOT wife of Andrew McVittie who died at Arkin 21st July 1879 aged 26 years   Also the above ANDREW THOMSON McVITTIE died 17th May 1923 aged 69 years (post 1950 inscription)

210 Sacred to the memory of WILLIAM BORTHWICK late a Colonel in the H.M. Indian Army who died at Longwood near Langholm on the 26th day of July 1867 in the 81st year of his age   Also in loving memory of MARIA ANNE MAXWELL of Longwood widow of Colonel Borthwick who entered her rest 8th March 1891 "I will give you rest" Matt.X1.28 "He will swallow up

death in victory" Isaiah XXV.8 (Left side of base) In remembrance
of WILLIAM DAVID MAXWELL BORTHWICK only son of
Colonel Borthwick who died at Longwood, Langholm 31st
December 1872 in his 30th year "Thou drewest near in the day
that I called upon thee: thou saidst fear not" Lam.3.57 (Right
side of base)   Also in loving memory of ELIZABETH HAY
BORTHWICK of Longwood only daughter of Colonel Borthwick
and widow of the the late James Milnes Stansfeld of Flockton
who entered into her rest 28th June 1903 aged 61 years (post
1950 inscription)

211   ISABELLA BELL BORTHWICK who died at Billholm, Westerkirk,
       on 1st May 1908

212   In memory of MARGARET SCOTT wife of Thomas Chalmers
       Borthwick, Hopsrig, Westerkirk, who died at Edinburgh 8th June
       1883 aged 72 years and THOMAS CHALMERS BORTHWICK
       late of Hopsrig who died at Milnholm, Langholm 16th December
       1888 aged 75 years   Also their son ALEXANDER HAY
       BORTHWICK who died at Langholm 11th October 1890 aged
       47 years

213   In memory of ELIZABETH JACKSON wife of Robert Telfer,
       Shepherd, who died at Glenrief 1st November 1877 aged 58
       years   Also the above ROBERT TELFER who died at Hawick
       19th December 1889 aged 70 years   Also their daughter
       MARGARET who died at 16 Gladstone Street, Hawick, on the
       2nd September 1928 aged 82 years   Also their daughter JANE
       who died at 16 Gladstone Street Hawick, 30th July 1939 aged 71
       years

214   In memory of JAMES McVITTIE Clogger, who died in Langholm
       22nd August 1879 aged 31 years   Also HELEN IRVING
       his wife who died 21st April 1910 aged 58 years   Also
       JOHN McVITTIE their son who died 13th March 1922 aged 47
       years

215   In loving memory of JOHN YOUNG who died at Langholm
       11th March 1917 aged 65 years   Also MARY McVITTIE
       his wife who died at Langholm 14th March 1919 aged 69
       years   Also MARY their daughter who died in infancy at
       Potholm

216   In memory of GEORGE COWAN, Shepherd, who died at
       Arkin 26th January 1911 in his 59th year   Also his wife
       MARY ELLIOT who died at Langholm 23rd April 1941 aged 90
       years

217   In memory of WALTER IRVING infant son of Andrew Irving
       and Euphemia Keen, Glendinning, who died at Bogfoot, Ewes
       6th April 1882 aged 4 months   Also MARGARET their
       daughter who died at Woolhope 29th November 1887 aged 7
       months   Also the above ANDREW IRVING who died at
       Park Cottage, Newcastleton 4th July 1929 aged 79 years   Also
       the above EUPHEMIA KEEN who died at Park Cottage,
       Newcastleton 19th April 1930 aged 79 years   Also ISABELLA
       their daughter who died at Flatt, Newcastleton 30th October 1948
       aged 63 years

218   Sacred to the memory of JOHN TELFER who died at Carretrigg
       on the 5th day of January 1879 aged 44 years   Also JANE
       OGILVIE his wife who died at 9 Doncaster Street, Newcastleton
       13th June 1915 aged 80 years   Also JANET OGILVIE their
       eldest daughter who died at 9 Doncaster Street, Newcastleton on
       27th June 1937 aged 76 years (post 1950 inscription)

219   In memory of HELEN McVITTIE wife of William Elliot who died
       at Westwater June 15th 1863 aged 40 years   Also JANET
       their daughter who died at Arkleton December 7th 1862 aged 10
       years   Also the above WILLIAM ELLIOT who died at
       Peelbraehope 17th December 1897 aged 77 years   Also
       CHARLOTTE his daughter who died in infancy   Also
       ROBERT YOUNG ELLIOT his son who died at Peelbraehope

9th April 1903 aged 20 years   Also ELIZABETH LITTLE wife of William Elliot who died at Newcastleton December 9th 1923 aged 77 years

220   In memory of JAMES JOHNSTON who died at Kirkstile 19th June 1889 aged 67 years   Also ISABELLA CARLYLE his wife who died at Beckhall, Canonbie 20th September 1895 aged 69 years   Also AGNES their daughter who died at Barrascroft, Canonbie 19th February 1893 aged 24 years

221   Erected in loving memory of ISABELLA LAUDER wife of John Johnston who died at Langholm 10th March 1902 aged 40 years   Also HELEN HUTTON LAUDER their niece who died 18th June 1903 aged 20 years

222   In loving memory of AGNES KIRKPATRICK wife of William Haining, Gamekeeper, Sykefoot, who died there 12th June 1911 aged 30 years   Also SAMUEL their son who died in infancy

223   In memory of ROBERT HARDIE, Farmer, who died at Sorbie 19th April 1858 aged 67 years   Also of HELEN PATERSON his wife who died at Sorbie 16th January 1859 aged 57 years   Also of WILLIAM FRANCIS HARDIE their son who died at Tunbridge Wells, Kent, 29th June 1860 aged 36 years Also JAMES HARDIE their son who died at Sorbie 10th March 1867 aged 35 years   Also JOHN HARDIE their son who died at Sorbie 1st May 1868 aged 32 years (inscribed age amended) Also HENRY HARDIE their son who died at London, Ontario, America 27th May 1876 aged 50 years   Also ROBERT HARDIE their son who died at Byreburnfoot, Canonbie, 31st August 1877 aged 37 years   Also DAVID HARDIE their son Tenant of Priesthaugh who died there 6th January 1889 aged 67 years   Also WALTER DOUGLAS HARDIE their son who died at Byreburnfoot 22nd November 1889 aged 59 years Also ISABELLA PATERSON HARDIE their daughter who died at Wavertree, Liverpool, 1st February 1891 aged 53 years

Also MARGARET SCOTT widow of David Hardie who died at Priesthaugh 29th December 1893 aged 67 years "The Lord gave and the Lord hath taken away blessed be the name of the Lord"

224 In memory of FRANCIS T. ANDERSON who died at Riggfoot 13th May 1945 aged 69 years   Also FRANK son of above who died at Burngrains 25th February 1913 aged 9m (post 1950 inscription)

225 In memory of WILLIAM DALZELL who died at Langholm 10th May 1883 aged 75 years   Also JANE TAIT his wife who died at Stablecleuch 23rd December 1882 aged 59 years

226 In memory of EDWARD ANDERSON son of Alexander and Elizabeth Anderson who died at Eweshaugh, Arkleton 26th June 1888 in his 17th year   Also ELIZABETH ANDERSON their grand daughter who died there 15th May 1888 aged 9 years   Also the above ELIZABETH A. HINDMARSH who died 14th September 1895 aged 69 years   Also the above ALEXANDER ANDERSON who died 10th January 1904 aged 83 years

227 In memory of ROBERT BEATTIE, Gamekeeper who died at Flaskholm September 1st 1864 aged 56 years   Also AGNES ARMSTRONG his spouse who died at Flaskholm December 12th 1873 aged 64 years   Also MARGARET BEATTIE their daughter who died at 4 Minto Place, Hawick 17th September 1903 aged 71 years

228 In memory of HENRIETTA FORREST wife of John Beattie who died at Stablecleuch on the 20th July 1885 aged 82 years   Also the above JOHN BEATTIE who died 21st February 1888 aged 79 years "All those that sleep in Jesus will God bring with him"   Also DAVID EDWARD FORREST BEATTIE their son who died at Georgetown, Demerara, U.S.A. 11th October 1889 aged 53 years

229   In affectionate remembrance of JANET GRAHAM wife of James Scott who died at Kirkstyle 6th December 1888 aged 36 years Also MARGARET HOGG his second wife who died 31st March 1893 aged 27 years   Also the above JAMES SCOTT who died at Kirkstyle 5th August 1924 aged 74 years (stone encrusted with hardened lichen)

230   In memory of FANNY BARTON wife of Andrew Armstrong , Gardener, who died at Arkleton 4th March 1890 aged 28 years

231   In memory of JAMES R. ROBSON son of John Robson and Janet Davidson who died at Glenrief 13th December 1890 aged 8 months and 3 weeks   Also ANNIE ROBSON their daughter wife of William Brockie who died at Rotheryhaugh 6th December 1906 aged 33 years   Also JANET DAVIDSON wife of the above John Robson who died at Glenrief 13th March 1908 aged 61 years   Also the above JOHN ROBSON who died at Langholm 25th July 1922 aged 80 years

232   In memory of MARGARET BEATTIE wife of Matthew Little who died at Howgill 3rd August 1902 aged 73 years   Also the above MATTHEW LITTLE late farmer in Howgill who died 14th April 1909 aged 80 years

233   In memory of JOHN YOUNG, ploughman who died at Staplegordon 16th April 1894 aged 77 years   Also JANET EWART his wife who died at Staplegordon 9th May 1896 aged 79 years   Also ALEXANDER their son who died at Broats 1848 aged 13 years and is interred in Dornock Churchyard MARY McLELLAN YOUNG wife of George Young their son who died at Langholm 24th September 1904 aged 54 years   Also the above GEORGE YOUNG who died 20th November 1919 aged 73 years (post 1950 inscription)

234   In memory of REBECCA DAVIDSON wife of Thomas Wilson who died at Ravanburn [sic] 19th March 1888 aged 33 years and

is interred in Canonbie Churchyard   Also JOHN JAMES their son who died at Hillhead 7th March 1889 aged 7 years Also JAMES STOREY step son of Thomas Wilson who died at Hamilton 6th December 1898 aged 17 years   Also JANET STOREY his second wife who died at Hillhead 22nd January 1904 aged 44 years

235   In loving memory of ANDREW BEATTIE, joiner who died at Langholm 10th January 1889 aged 53 years   Also MARGARET BEATTIE his wife who died 19th February 1909 aged 73 years

236   In memory of JANET IRVINE, a native of Bowden, Roxburghshire who died at Bush, Ewes 30th May 1862 aged 61 years

237   In loving memory of THOMAS McVITTIE, Roadman who died at Townhead, Langholm 25th December 1901 aged 71 years Also MARION BYERS his wife who died 29th September 1920 aged 93 years   Also ROBERT their son who died at Dumbarton 17th July 1927 aged 65 years interred in Alexandria Cemetery.   Also JANE MAGGIE their daughter who died 22nd May 1934 aged 63 years

238   In loving memory of HELEN HENRY wife of Adam Crozier who died at Kirton, March 8th 1926 aged 56 years (post 1950 inscription)

239   In memory of JANE ROGAN wife of David Anderson who died at Riggfoot, 24th September 1934 aged 78 years   Also DAVID ANDERSON who died 4th July 1936 aged 71 years

240   In memory of JAMES POTTS son of John Potts and Elizabeth Murray who died at Barngliesh-March 6th August 1874 aged 19 years   Also WILLIAM POTTS their son who died 11th September 1874 aged 14 years   Also JOHN M. POTTS their

son who died at Nubie [sic] 17th June 1875 aged 21 years
Also ELIZABETH MURRAY his wife who died at Nubie 22nd
September 1878 aged 32 years　　Also the above JOHN POTTS
who died at Nubie 26th May 1880 aged 54 years　　Also
ISABELLA POTTS their daughter who died in Langholm 10th
May 1882 aged 22 years　　Also ESTER [sic] POTTS their
daughter who died on board the ship Collin Grove 23rd November
1883 aged 25 years

241　In loving memory of JOHN CAMPBELL who died at Kirkstyle
24th February 1926 aged 75 years　　Also his wife
CATHERINE BELL who died at Kirkstyle 26th February 1942
aged 87 years　　Also two sons of the above who were killed in
France PTE. WILLIAM CAMPBELL 8th Gordon Hds. 30th
March 1916 aged 21 years　　Also PTE. DAVID CAMPBELL
1st April 1917 aged 19 years　　Also MARY AGNES HUNTER
granddaughter of the above who died at Kirkstyle 23rd June 1920
aged 3 years and 3 months (post 1950 inscription)

242　In loving memory of JOHN HOGG who died at Kirkstyle May
27th 1928 aged 61 years　　Also MARTHA McGLASSON his
wife who died at Thomas Hope Hospital August 18th 1936 aged
71 years　　Also PTE. THOMAS HOGG their son, of the 4th/
5th Battalion K.O.S.B. who was killed in France 1st August 1918
aged 24 years

243　In loving memory of MARGARET TURNBULL who died at
Glenrief, Ewes, August 17th 1928 aged 64 years　　Also DAVID
TURNBULL father of the above who died at Riggfoot, Ewes May
9th 1921 aged 92 years interred in Maxton Churchyard　　Also
MARY WHITSON daughter of above who died at Stablecleuch
February 28th 1944 aged 83 years

244　In loving memory of MARY MARGARET died at Arkletonshiels
23rd October 1940 aged 13 years (daughter of Robert Hyslop
and Mary Grieve) (post 1950 inscription).

245 In loving memory of WILLIAM CAMPBELL who died at Stablecleuch, Ewes May 9th 1937 aged 77 years Also MARGARET NICHOLSON wife of the above who died at Redcliffe Rd., Manchester, October 10th 1891 aged 35 years interred in Hoddam Churchyard

246 Sacred to the memory of AGNES WARD beloved wife of John Donaldson who died at The Burn, Westerkirk, 15th August 1937 aged 66 years   Also the above JOHN DONALDSON who died at The Burn, Westerkirk 26th September 1940 aged 66 years

247 In memory of CHRISTIAN HYSLOP wife of Christopher Oliver who died at Swingle 24th August 1885 aged 41 years   Also the above CHRISTOPHER OLIVER, Shepherd, who died at Swingle 17th October 1908 aged 65 years (post 1950 inscriptions)

248 To the memory of HENRY OLIVER, Shepherd, Swingle who died 16th January 1862 aged 47 years   Also AGNES C. NICHOLSON his wife who died at Brieryshaw Cottage 22nd May 1888 aged 78 years   Also their daughter JANE OLIVER who died at Swingle 22nd April 1921 aged 79 years

249 In memory of JAMES TELFOR [sic] Shepherd, who died at Mosspeeble 21st July 1895 aged 40 years   Also JANE BUCHANAN his wife who died at 33 Townhead St. Lockerbie 27th October 1904 aged 42 years

250 In memory of DAVID MOFFAT McVITTIE son of Henry McVittie and Mary Moffat who died at Henwell 31st October 1896 aged 9 years and 1 months   Also the said HENRY McVITTIE Shepherd who died at Langholm 28th October 1901 aged 48 years   Also the above MARY MOFFAT died at Langholm 28th January 1935 aged 81 years (post 1950 inscription)

251 In memory of GEORGE KENEDY [sic] who died at Fiddleton 4th January 1897 aged 41 years   Also HELEN TURNBULL

his wife who died at Causewood, Midlothian, 26th May 1940 aged 81 years   Also WILLIAM KENNEDY their son who fell in action in France 9th April 1917 aged 28 years (post 1950 inscription)

252   In loving memory of NELLIE wife of Thomas Jackson who died at Bogfoot, Ewes July 15th 1921 aged 76 years   Also the above THOMAS JACKSON who died at Bogfoot on his 92nd birthday August 19th 1931

253   In loving memory of WILLIAM DAVIDSON who died at Mosspeeble Cottage January 17th 1922 aged 75 years   Also JANE DAVIDSON wife of above who died at Fleety, Heriot February 10th 1947 aged 88 years

254   Ever remembering JOHN (JOCK) WELCH JOHNSTONE PATERSON born at Terrona 6th July 1921 died there 20th October 1928 son of James John (Jimmy) Paterson (post 1950 inscriptions)

255   In memory of JAMES ELLIOT of Burnfoot who died 9th December 1947 aged 67 years (post 1950 inscriptions)

256   In memory of MARGARET FERGUSON ELLIOT wife of James Douglas who died at Unthank 19th September 1949 aged 71 years (post 1950 inscription)

257   In memory of JOHN CONNOR who having lived some time in the family of William Welsh at Wrae returned to Burnfoot on Esk where he died much regretted 28th January 1835 aged 18 "Hath not God chosen the poor of this world rich in faith"

258   In loving memory of JOHN IRVINE who died at Greenhead, Langholm, 3rd July 1902 aged 61 years   Also his son JOHN who died in infancy   Also CLEMENTINA HOGG his wife who died at Langholm 26th May 1914 aged 70 years

Ewes Index

*Two views
of
Unthank Burial Ground*

3

*Memorials in
Unthank Churchyard*

1 Here lyes WILLIAM ELLIOT, tenant in Broadlee who died 30th
_____ 1767 aged 89 years   Also ISABEL SCOTT his spouse
daughter of John Scott in Falnash who died 26th _____ 1769
aged 89 years   Also WILLIAM their son, tenant in Broadlee
who died February 8th 1771 aged __ 60?   Also JOHN ELLIOT
of Whithaugh his eldest son who died _____ 1778 aged 76? years
Also MARGARET SCOTT his spouse daughter of Scott of
Gorinberry who died 2nd May 1768 aged 64 ? years   Also four
of their children MARGARET, ISABELLA, MARY and WALTER
who died young.   William Elliot of Whithaugh's spouse
MARGARET SHORTREED, daughter of Robert Shortreed of
Esk__side who died December 18th 1778 aged 48 years   Also
said WILLIAM ELLIOT who died March 1776 aged 50 years
Also ELIZABETH ELLIOT his sister who died (uncut year and
age) Also ISABELLA ELLIOT his sister who died July 1807 aged
75 years   Also THOMAS ELIOT (sic) his brother, tenant in
Twiselhope who died October 4th 1807 aged 77 years   Also
ISABELLA ELLIOT his daughter who died October 29th 1808
aged 43 (or 48) years   Also JEAN ELLIOT daughter of
Robert Elliot of Binks spouse to John Elliot of Whithaugh who
died June 22nd 1787 aged 29 years   Also two children who died
in infancy   Also JAMES ELLIOT, merchant in Hawick, son of

William Elliot of Whithaugh who died April 28th 1824 aged 55 ? years   Also MARGARET ELLIOT his daughter who died at Glengirtholm 11th August 1837 aged 82 years   Also JANE ELLIOT his daughter who died there September 2nd 1838 aged 81 years   Also WILLIAM ELLIOT his son who died at Newcastleton 25th February 1843 aged 80 years   Also JOHN ELLIOT Esq. Whithaugh eldest son of above William Elliot who died 3rd May 1847 aged 88 years (Superscription on memorial – ELLIOTS OF WHITHAUGH)

NOTE: This memorial, a table tomb, is parallel to that of Robert Elliot, son to John Elliot of Whithaugh, and this fact has enabled the provision of "estimated dates" shown underlined for first inscriptions on the memorial.   Unfortunately, the inscriptions were virtually indecipherable, except for an odd age, due to encrustation of hardened lichen.   The estimates are thought to be reasonable, taking into account the statement that John Elliot of Whithaugh was the eldest son.   Also the definite ages and dates of later generations.

2   In memory of ROBERT ELLIOT, tenant in Hermitage who died 11th December 1858 aged 67 years   Also MARY ELLIOT his spouse daughter of Thomas Murray, Whisgill who died 8th March 1835 aged 31 years   Also THOMAS ELLIOT their son who died at Scoor, Island of Mull, 4th November 1854 aged 24 years

3   Here lyes JANET THOMSON spouse to Adam Laidlow in Fidleton Bar 21st July 1777 aged 63 years   Also five children Also aforesaid ADAM LAIDLOW who died at Fidleton Bar November 24th 1780 aged 75 years

4   Erected in memory of ROBERT LAIDLAW late tenant in Gorrinberry who died January 8th 1815 in the 77th year of his age

5   Here lyes ROBERT ELLIOT son to John Elliot of Whithaugh who died at Millburnholm February 10th 1770 aged 45 years Also JANET SCOTT his spouse who died July 1774 aged 43 years   Also CHRISTIAN GRIVE (sic) spouse to John Elliot their son, she died at Millburnholm 27th December 1783 aged 30 years   Also WALTER ELLIOT his son who died at Hermitage November 20th 1797 aged 43 (or 45)   Also JOHN ELLIOT tenant in Deadwater son of above Robert Elliot who died 10th June 1821 aged 71 years   Also ELIZABETH LAIDLAW spouse to William Elliot, tenant in Millburnholm son of above Robert Elliot who died November 25th 1822 aged 72 years   Also said WILLIAM ELLIOT tenant in Millburnholm who died 31st June 1827 aged 77 years   Also JOHN ELLIOT son of above John Elliot who died at Netherhindhope 21st January 1833 aged 37 years   Also JOHN ELLIOT tenant in Templehall, son of William Elliot who died at Hawick 22nd November 1834 aged 38 years   Also HELEN CROZIER wife of above Walter Elliot who died at Hermitage 15th March 1854 aged 84 years

6   Sacred to the memory of ROBERT ELLIOT second son of William Elliot, Esq. of Whithaugh, who died at Glengirtholm 17th March 1840 aged 79 years   Also ALISON GREIG his relict who died at Clinthead 5th May 1856 aged 77 years

7   In memory of ANDREW ELLIOT, farmer in Twislop (sic) who died 28th June 1866 aged 79 years

8   In memory of ROLAND ELIOT, farmer in Mackside who died there 10th March 1847 aged 31 years   Also BEATRIX POTT his spouse who died at Wilton Hill, Hawick 13th December 1878 aged 79 years

9   In memory of JAMES ELLIOT, tenant in Lymiecleugh who died 24th May 1850 aged 66 years   Also ELIZABETH ELLIOT his spouse who died 12th October 1833 aged 46 years   Also of

their children: SCOTT ELLIOT who died 1st April 1824 aged 8 years   Also JAMES ELLIOT who died 27th May 1827 aged 13 years   Also ELIZABETH ELLIOT who died 5th January 1835 aged 15 years   Also JAMES ELLIOT who died 2nd May 1843 aged 15 years

10   In memory of WILLIAM ELLIOT, shepherd in Hartsgarth who perished in the River Kershope October 17th 1824 aged 54 years Also JEAN EASTON his spouse who died at Longhaugh 25th April 1834 aged 57 years   Also their son WILLIAM ELLIOT who died at Newcastleton 27th April 1830 aged 17 years

11   In memory of BARBARY (sic) ELLIOT daughter to James Elliot in Twislehope who died 11th January 1792 aged 18 years   Also ROLLAND ELLIOT son who died 7th July 1799 aged 33 years Also KATHRINE LITTLE his spouse who died at Newcastleton November 1808 aged 44 years

12   In memory of ELIZABETH JACKSON spouse of James Elliot herd at Twislehope June 29th 1806 aged 62 years   Also JAMES ELLIOT who died 1st April 1816 aged 83 years

13   In memory of JANE ELLIOT relict of James Bogie born 28th February 1757 died 9th September 1838

14   Here lyes GAVIN WILKIE who died at Meikledalehaugh 1st June 1720 aged 48 years   Also MARY ELLIOT his spouse who died 15th February 1762 aged 89 years   Also ROBERT WILKIE his son who died in Houpasley 30th April 1760 aged 48 years

15   Here lyes JOHN ELLIOT who died March 28th 1704 his age one year and 5 months   Also ADAM ELLIOT who died November 2nd 1724 aged 22 years   Also NINION (sic) ELLIOT who died February 23rd 1724 aged 27 years

16   Top of memorial inscribed : 1661 : JOHN ELLIOT late in Dinly
      who died at Park 28th December 1728 aged 78 years   Also
      WILLIAM ELLIOT his son who died at Park 29th January 1791
      aged 88 years   Also HELEN SCOT his spouse who died
      December 22nd 1774 aged 72 years   Also JOHN ELLIOT
      tenant in Byegate who died 11th August 1808 aged 77 years

17   (Fragment reading of indecipherable stone) _____ also HENRY ?
      ELLIOT tenant in _____ 1731 ? age 107

18   Here lyes JOHN THOMSON in Mospeble [sic] who died October
      27th 1738 aged 76 years   Also JENET ELIOT his spouse who
      died July 28th 1739 age 70 years

19   In memory of ANDREW NICHOL, Shepherd in Burnfoot who
      died 9th May 1815 aged 57 years   Also JEAN ELLIOT his
      spouse who died 24th September 1834 aged 78 years

20   Heir lyes ADAM ELIOT of Meikledale who died August 16th
      1682 aged 82 years. NOTE: Historical Monuments (Scotland
      Commission) record this table stone as located at the South West
      end of the foundation of the original Church

21   Here lyes ROBERT ANDERSON in Carritrige who died October
      25, 1707 his age 63 years

22   Here lyes WILLIAM HUTTON late merchant in Sudhope who
      died 1st February 1764 aged 82 years   Also JEAN SCOT his
      spouse who died October 26th 1750 aged 58 years

23   In memory of ADAM GREIVE who died at Cheplehill 14th July
      1849 aged 75 years   Also MARGARET PATERSON his spouse
      who died March 14th 1866 aged 80 years

24   (A table stone copiously inscribed but indecipherable in view of
      hardened lichen encrustations) – initial text opens – Here lyes

ROBERT SCOTT tenant in _____ (possibly Broadlee, the date could be October 1753 aged 71 but this should be accepted with reserve)

25   ROBERT NICHOL, tenant in Philhope who died March 15th 1803 aged 64 years

26   Here lyes JOHN NICOL son to Robert Nicol late herd in Burngrains who died 14th October 1742 aged 27 years   Also MARY BEATY his spouse who died 14th January 1781 aged 66 years

27   In memory of ANDREW BYERS in Unthank who died Aprile 1747 aged 88 years

28   In memory of ANDREW BYERS farmer in High Stenries who died 17th November 1850 aged 64 years   Also MARY ROGERSON spouse to Andrew Byers in High Stenries who died 25th June 1848 aged 53 years   Also JANET BYERS their daughter who died 15th August 1834 aged 18 years

29   In memory of MICHAEL BYERS son to James Byers in High Stoneridge who died 21st March 1791 aged 18 years   Also CHRISTIAN BYERS his daughter who died 1st February 1812 aged 19 years   Also above JAMES BYERS tenant in High Stoneridge who died 31st October 1824 aged 79 years   Also MARGARET LITTLE his spouse who died at High Stoneridge January 27th 1828 aged 77 years   Also WILLIAM BYERS surgeon son of above James Byers who died at Broadmeadow 11th August 1872 aged 90 years

30   In memory of WILLIAM BYERS in Craig who died 18th January 1781 aged 65 years   Also ELEZABETH [sic] COWAN his spouse who died in Ewislees 29th March 1766 aged 51 years

31   Here lyes JAMES BYERS who died April 2nd 1746 aged 82 years Also JEAN ARMSTRONG his spouse who died 6th February

1750 aged 80 years   Also BETTY ARMSTRONG spouse to Richart (sic) Byers who died 30th March 1750 aged 28 years Also ISABEL their daughter who died April 7th 1750 aged 2 years

32   In memory of RICHARD BYERS who died in Burn 28th March 1783 aged 72 years   Also ISOBEL COUAN (sic) his spouse who died in Craig December 24th 1786 aged 76 years (the six of 76 is cross cut and could be a 4) MICHAEL BYERS who died at Highstaneridge 23rd March 1824 aged 76 years   Also CHRISTIAN BYERS who died at Highstaneridge 17th November 1823 aged 81 years

33   Here lyes JOHN ANDERSON shepherd in Lodgegill who died December 11th 1788 aged 63 years   Also ROBERT his son who died 12th December 177- aged 15 months   Also GEORGE who died April 15th 1779 aged 16 years

34   Intered here remains of ADAM HOWISON, Mosspeople [sic] who died 13th April 1759 aged 50 years   Also JANET ROBSON his spouse who died 29th June 1747 (no age cut)   Also JOHN HOWISON their son who died 24th December 1758 aged 14 years   Also JANET who died 16th November 1764 aged 17 years   Also ANDREW who died 21st November 1758 aged 5 years

35   In memory of JOHN LAWSON of Knittyholm who died 24th June 1800 aged 73 years   Also AGNES SCOTT his spouse who died 10th May 1778 aged 53 years   Also ELIZABETH MURRAY second spouse who died 21st February 1816 aged 73 years   Also JAMES LAWSON his son who died in Belfast 29th November 1782 aged 27 years   Also ROBERT LAWSON his son who died 2nd October 1793 aged 27 years   Also CAPTAIN JOHN LAWSON his son who died in middle passage from Africa to West Indies 19th December 1804 aged 45 years Also JAMES LAWSON second son of that named who died in Demerara, West Indies March 1805 aged 18 years

36 (Reverse of 35) ANDREW LAWSON who died at Crofthead 4th October 1844 aged 62 years   Also CHARLOTTE MARTIN his wife who died at Hollows 15th June 1867 aged 84 years

37 In memory of ROBERT McVITTIE who died at Fidleton 8th August 1873 aged 82 years   Also his wife JANE JACKSON who died at Fidleton 3rd January 1838 aged 48 years   Also JAMES their son who died November 18th 1843 aged 26 years   Also MARGARET daughter of Robert McVittie and Janet Armstrong who died 20th March 1865 aged 13 years Also said JANET ARMSTRONG his second wife who died at Priesthaugh Cottage 19th February 1897 aged 75 years

38 In memory of JAMES LAIDLAW who died at New Langholm March 26th 1787 aged 78 years   Also CHRISTIAN ARMSTRONG his spouse who died June 8th 1748 aged 37 years Also HELEN LAIDLAW their daughter who died September 1814 aged 78 years

39 In memory of JOHN JACKSON who died at Sandyhaugh March 11th 1835 aged 84 years   Also HELEN LAIDLAW his spouse who died there September 3rd 1804 aged 49 years   Also four   children who died in infancy   Also ELIZABETH RUNCIMAN his second spouse who died February 14th 1858 aged 83 years

40 This stone is erected by Jane Duncan in Bilholmburn to the memory of her husband HENRY JACKSON who died at Langholm January 10th 1825 aged 28 years   Also HELEN JACKSON their daughter who died November 10th 1824 aged 2 years and 5 months Likewise 2 sons who died in infancy

41 Sacred to the memory of MARGARET SCOTT wife of William Turnbull in Falnash who died 5th April 1845 aged 34 years (Post 1855 inscriptions)

42 In memory of DAVID BEATTIE who died at Hawkhass 3rd March 1852 aged 53 years   Also JAMES their son who died at Hawkhass February 1846 aged 17 years   Also ELIZABETH their daughter who died at Wisp in October 1839 aged 9 years (no wife stated)

43 _____ here   Also ROBERT SCOT who died March 17th 1729 his age 31 years (further inscriptions too deeply embedded)

44 In memory of JAMES NICOLL who died in Langholm who died May 27th 1815 aged 67 years   Also EUPHEMIA GRIEVE his spouse who died 11th November 1825 aged 68 years

45 In memory of ROBERT NICOL who died in January 5th 1779 aged 73 years   Also his wife ANN ARMSTRONG who died in Arkeltown December __ 1747 aged 55 years   Also five children who died in infancy   Also of his wife MARGARET POTT who died April 1779 aged 78 years

46 In memory of JAMES BYERS who died in New Langholm __ May 1787 aged 88 years

Memorials in the walled enclosure in Unthank Burial Ground

47 In memory of MARGARET ATCHISON, daughter of Robert Atchison, Mosspeeble who died 15th December 1789 aged 21 years   Also the above ROBERT ATCHISON who died 21st July 1799 aged 61 years And JEAN ATCHISON his sister who died 15th December 1799 aged 46 years

48 Here lies EDWARD ATCHISON tenant in Deweslays who died 3rd December 1726 aged 81 years JANE ELLIOT his spouse who

died 3rd April 1726 aged 61 years and their children MARGARET,
MARY and MARGARET died in infancy DAVID aged 6 years
EDWARD aged 4 years   WILLIAM ATCHISON, tenant in
Deweslays who died 22nd June 1727 aged 30 years

49   In memory of WILLIAM ATCHISON, late in Burnfoot who died
     24th November 1794 aged 77 years BEATRIX ELLIOT his spouse
     who died 30th March 1764 aged 41 years WILLIAM ATCHISON
     their son who died 25th June 1836 aged 78 years MARY POTT
     his spouse who died April 1856 aged 88 years   Also their son
     GEORGE POTT ATCHISON tenant in Mount Benger who died
     25th June 1853 aged 49 years (later inscriptions)

50   Here lies ROBERT ATCHISON, Tenant in Deweslays who died
     18th June 1728 aged 47 years JANET ATCHISON who died
     18th November 1714 aged 2__ years and JANET ATCHISON
     who died 22nd September 1726 aged 2 months both children of
     Robert Atchison and CHRISTIAN CARMICHAEL, his spouse,
     who died 10th December 1746 aged 63 years   Also CHRISTIAN
     ELLIOT, spouse to Edward Atchison, late tenant in Eweslies who
     died 16th November 1764 aged 52 years   Also MARGARET
     ATCHISON their daughter who died 22nd November 1764 aged
     24 years   Also the above EDWARD ATCHISON who died at
     Mosspeeble 14th March 1781 aged 60?

51   In memory of CHARLES ATCHISON, Unthank who died 22nd
     July 1795 aged 39 years   Also MARGARET SCOTT his
     spouse who died 18th April 1827 aged 67 years   Also
     MARGARET ATCHISON their daughter who died 7th February
     1812 aged 19 years   Also CHARLES ATCHISON their son
     who died 10th February 1847 aged 57 years (later inscriptions)

Unthank Index

4

_᎔᎕_

1867–1967
Centenary Leaflet

T he Church in Ewes, dedicated to St Cuthbert, is of pre-
Reformation origin and, while it is not possible accurately to
date its formation, reference is made to an incumbency in 1187.
The present Ewes Kirk is the only remaining one – the Nether Kirk – of
the three or possibly four that at one time existed in the parish. The
building, the second on the same site and rather bigger than it pre-
decessor, was opened on 13th October 1867. The bell in the tree, an
unusual and distinctive feature, was taken from the former building
and still calls the people to worship.

The Church has had notable ministries in a notable history. During
Covenanting times the Rev. John Lythgow was removed from his charge
in 1664 and, having refused "to stop preaching the Gospel", was
imprisoned in the Bass Rock. The long and distinguished ministry of
the Rev. Robert Malcolm from 1717 till 1761 is a memorable record.
The monument to his grandson, General Sir John Malcolm, one of the
"Knights of Eskdale", rises from the top of Whita Hill and can be seen
at a great distance over a wide area.

When the new Church was built and opened in 1867, the Rev. Thomas
Smith had already been minister for fifteen years and he continued in
office for a further thirty-eight years. He was succeeded by the Rev.
David Preston, during whose ministry of seventeen years the present
organ was installed, thus superseding the precentor in leading the people's

praise. During this period also the Woman's Guild was formed. The tradition of long incumbencies was maintained by the Rev. John Kerr who ministered for thirty-seven years with great acceptance, endearing himself not only to his parishioners but also to many others beyond the bounds of the parish. During his pastorale the pulpit was moved to the side and the present chancel with the central Communion Table was formed. The old preceptor's desk is preserved for use as a lectern and the collecting "ladles" together with the former gate for "fencing the Tables" are set along the walls. The Communion Table, Communion Plate, Alms Plate and Font are memorial gifts, while the lovely Pulpit Fall and embroidered Bible-markers are the gift of Mrs. Kerr in memory of her late husband.

1867–1967 Ewes Church Building Centenary Celebrations

The Parish of Ewes had already been linked with that of Westerkirk when the present minister, the Rev. J. J. Glover, was inducted by the Presbytery of Hawick to the combined charge in 1956. The usual Church life continues as before except for the very popular "Sunday" school which meets on Fridays under the instruction of the Minister and Mrs. Glover.

The Kirk depends for its effectiveness upon the quality of its elders and this has been eminently true of Ewes Kirk. During the past century J. C. Little (Burnfoot), T. Lyle (Schoolhouse) and J. B. Robertson (Arkleton) have left an honoured name, while the present Kirk Session comprising I. Dalgliesh (Glendivan), W. Hislop (Hoghill), D. Irving (Brieryshaw), D. Scott (Treasurer, of Arkin) and T. Scott (Eweslees) maintain in devotion and zeal the highest tradition.

Spiritually and financially the Woman's Guild has played an invaluable part and in the hands of Mrs. Glover (President), Mrs Dalgliesh (Secretary) and Mrs. D. Scott (Treasurer) continues to do so.

Many changes have taken place in the life and character of the parish but the Church remains, the undying witness to the Gospel, the spiritual home and home-maker of the people, the training ground for character and service. In spite of the difficulties of country life today she pulses at the heart of the parish and the faithful nucleus labour on in faith and love, grateful for Divine blessing in the past, hopeful for its continuance in the future.

Ewes Church looking toward the North

5

Ministers of Ewes Parish

WILLIAM GRAHAM, A.M.	1617
_____ CHISHOLM	(unrecorded)
JOHN LITHGOW	1646–1664
JOHN HOME, A.M.	166–
JOHN MELVILL, A.M.	168–
JOHN LITHGOW	1688–1694
ROBERT DARLING	1694–1716
ROBERT MALCOLM, A.M.	1717–1761
RICHARD SCOTT	1761
JOHN CLUNIE	1790
JOHN LAURIE	1791–1817
ROBERT SHAW	1817–1853
THOMAS SMITH	1853
DAVID PRESTON, B.D.	1901
JOHN ALEXANDER KERR, M.A., C.F.	1918–1955
J. JAMIESON GLOVER, M.A.	1956-1973

(Ewes linked with Westerkirk)

Memento Mori – tucked under a tree in Ewes is Memorial 113 –
James Easton son of John Easton in Hawick who died at Burnfoot.
Erected by his uncle Wm Easton.

6

Ewes Valley
Register of Testaments

(FROM THE COMMISSARIOT RECORD OF DUMFRIES COUNTY)

AINSLY Anna, relict of Wm. Elliot of Arkletoun	17/1/1733
ARMSTRONG Adam in Tarrona	14/8/1679
ARMSTRONG George in Wrae (thereafter in Langholm)	24/1/1775
ARMSTRONG Janet spouse to Wm. Little in Burnfoot	18/7/1684
ARMSTRONG John of Sorbie	3/5/1687
ARMSTRONG Margaret in Mosspeebles	5/8/1657
ARMSTRONG Thomas in Billholm	20/2/1752
BELL James in Kilburne	23/2/1676
ELLIOT Adam in Mickledale	16/7/1684
ELLIOT Archibald in Bintshawe	14/8/1679
ELLIOT Grissell spouse to Ninian Armstrong in Wrae	17/7/1656
ELLIOT Ninian in Bankend of Ewes	30/10/1685
ELLIOT Ninian in Dewflies (? Ewislees)	19/7/1661
ELLIOT Ninian in Milnsteed	28/11/1748
ELLIOT Walter of Arkleton	18/11/1717
ELLIOT William of Arkleton	16/5/1722 – 29/1/1724

GLENDONING James in Meikleholm or New Langholm　1789

HALL Mary, residenter in Bridgend of Ewes　15/11/1759

HOPE David, late in Becks thereafter in Wrae　6/8/1739

McVITIE Helen spouse to John Elliot in Glendivine　17/4/1685

MALCOLM Mr. Robert, Minister at Ewes　20/6/1763

MELVIL Thomas at Ewes Manse　5/2/1739

MURRAY William, weaver in Terrona　17/1/1733

ELLIOT Adam in Crocksbankhead　Jan. 1706

ELLIOT Walter of Arkleton　(July 1703–Aug.1707)　Oct. 1710

FISHER William, schoolmaster in Ewes Kirk　June 1715

McVITIE Jean spouse to Christopher Armstrong in Bushe　14/8/1679

BORTHICK Bessie in Carritrig　5/8/1657

ELLIOT Thomas in Byreburnside　19/3/1739

SCOTT William in Dueslees only lawful son to deceased
William Scott tenant in Falnesh　28 July 1730

The actual Register and Wills are available for public viewing at the Legal Search Department of the General Register Office, 2 Princes Street, Edinburgh: the ones on this list for Ewes have been extracted from the full Register

7

_ᏮᏮ_

Pardoned, or Amnesty List

TRANSCRIBED FROM AN ACT OF PARLIAMENT IN THE REIGN OF JAMES VI
A.D. 1585

The following is an extract from an Act of Parliament in favour of John Maxwell, Earl of Morton, his friends and servants. In the Act reference is made to the amnesty granted to Lord Hamilton Archibald, Earl of Angus and John Earl of Mar which was extended to Earl of Morton and his friens for the raid of Stirling. The pardon antedates to April 1569. The following parties were included with Lord John Maxwell of ? Munches, Eskdale and Carthill ? Kirtle.

Robert Maxwell of Castlemilk, his brother, the Baillies, Counsal and Commissaries of Dumfries and Annand, David brother to Sir Robert Maxwell of Dinwoodie, Kght – George Carruthers of Holmendis and the hail companies of Horsemen listed by him. Edward Maxwell of the Isle, Herbert Maxwell of Cavins, Robert Maxwell of Keltonn, Thomas Edgar in Bowhouses, John Brown in Land, Waltr Gledstanes, Craigs, Sir Robert Maxwell of Spot, Kght. John Maxwell of Newland, his brother and the hale companies of Horsemen listed by him. Capt. John, Richert and Wm. Maxwells and Captain Jas. Fraser, their Lieutenants, Ensigns and Officers and hail company of footmen listed by them. John Maxwell in Balgradden, Alexander Maxwell in Logan his son, Chas. Murray in Dalcohuick, James Hunter Drummschynock, John Lindsay, Auchinsketh, Jas. Charteris, Yr. Of Kilwood, Sit Alexr. Jardine,

Applegarth, Knyht. Jas. Douglas of Drumlanrigg, Edward Maxwell of Lamreglour, Wm. Dunbar of Blantyre, James Lindsay of Fairgarth even their hail kin and friends, men, tennants, servants, vassals, and dependaires, and all other Noble, Knichts, Barones, and gentlemen, landit and unlandit, Yeamen and Common that has under communal favour, assisted or given supplies to the said Earl whose names if not included in present Act salle be given up in a sufficient inventory be the Earls ane hand to the Clerk of the Reg; for their better Securety Act after revoking previous acts of forfeiture on parties confirms the Earldom of Morton to Maxwell.

For Annandale *see* Dalton Memorials.

Here follows a list of the parties referred to in the said Act :

Eskdale, Ewesdale and Wauchopedale

Dauid baty in blakesk – alie – rowe – hew – Jon and dauid batyis his sonis – andro baty in blakesk – archie and niniane batyis there – niniane ewart there – James thomesone there – Thome Scot there – willie and robie batyis thair – lowrie pot there – Dauid Dalgleis in wotcariok – Dauid baty there – Jame achesone there – ade glendonig there – adie grahame and Dauid baty in cauldkin – Jon and wat batyis his brether – Jhoun baty of burne sone to Adame – hew – John – geordier – Jinkin – wattie – and ade batyis the said Johns brether Jame baty – mugois (Mungo's) Jame in killclewis – wattie and migo (mungo) batyis his sonis – Jon Batie sone to migo in ronelburne – wattie – Rowe and thome batyis his brither Jon batie sone to arthor – Jon baty in carlisgill – geordie – nikie – Dauid – wattie – Sime and wat batyis and Jok – andro – Jame – Jok – Andro batyis there – adame baty in zetbyre – charlie batie there – mathew baty his sone – Jame baty thair – nikie baty in quhithauch – robe baty there – robe baty in byre – Sim baty and mathew batie sone to lang andro – geordie and andro baties – Steine – Sim and Dauid bateyis thrie brether. Wat batie of the Scheill – Jok batie his brother – Dauid and neke batyis tua brether – Jhonn batie in bank heid – Jon baty – braid Jon batie of the corfs – andro – Sandie and wattie bateis thre brether – Jon batie- his man Jok batie sone to the bra andro batie sone to trurie – adie batie his brother – Jon batie in glenbervell – Jon glendonig crowner – Jon glendonig afs Selhour – Jon batie of davingtoun – Jon – willie – wattie -geordie – bobbie bateis sonis to the said Jon – robe – Joke – Jon – peter – andro and hew bateis- Joke glespie – adie littill – andro baty sone to hew – Dauid – nicoll and Jok aitkins – Jon rae – christe and Joke litillis – Jame bennet – Thome rae – Jok ranik – Jame Jok and Syme brigis (Burgis) – ade thomsone – Rowe m'crie – Sym m'crie – naving baty – Jon aitkine – Jon glendonig – Jon Dagles – andro baty – edut (Edward) – Jon and Sym thomsonis – Jon thomsone – als rowll – Jon – peter and Jame betyis – Dik and will thomsonis – geordie and wattie batyis – Jhonn batie als nekeis – Jhonn – archie – nekie – adame – wattie and Dauid baties – alie batie in trowhoillis – andro batie his brother – Jon and Jame glendonigis – Jon haliday – mathew glendonig in castelhill – arche glendonig and Rowe baty in wester ker – criftie – archie and willie batyis – Jhonn broun in croisdykis – Jhonn brown – young peter glendonig – peter grahame – Jok glendonig – wattie crek – Jhonn batie in milgill – bartill glendonig – Syme glendonig – andro baty – Syme Scot – Syme baty – nikie Scot – willie banet – Jon boy – Jhonn Litill – george grahame in currutheris park – andro grahame his brother – wattie and thome grahames there – Jhonne bek – Jon Bell and Richie Bell in Hottis – nicoll moffett – adame haliday – ranie bell – Jhonn batie of the linholme – andro batie his s'vand – thome batie of the lynholme his brother – Jhonn bell thair – Row batie thair – nikie batie thair – Thome litill elder in the cuill – thome litill younger – Jon – andro and mathew litillis – nekie litle in Dalduran – jok – andro – Sym – archie clemet and dauid litillis thair – Jon and Jok litillis thair – pait litill in craigmekle – wat litill in Stankgait – wat litill thair – Jon litill in fingland – Rowe – Jame – Alexr – Andro and Syme littilis thair – Jhone litill in burnefute geordie litle thair – Cuddy litill in Stabilgortoun – andro – willie and wattie litillis thair – Jon litle in pollorane – archie litle in potholme – adie litill in dowglen – nike litill in milholme – wattie and francie litillis his sonis – Rowe litill thair – Rowe litill callit archies rowe – thome litill thair – Syme litill thair – Syme litill in bankhead – Nikie litle in brekcanwray – andro litle thair – archie litill thair – rowe litill and Dauid litill in clois – Jon th me t – persell litillis and mathowis – Jhonn litill thair – Dauid and Jok litles thair – andro litill sone to wat – wat litill in Igill – Rowe litill thair – Jhonn Irving in ower dowglen – richie and christie Irvingis thair – Brattill Irving in dowglencleuch – Dauid Jok and Alex Irvingis thair – cristie armestrang in barnegleish – Jhonn murray his man – christie murray – andro carrutis – thome bell – rot halyday – will bell and s Jhonne litill – Jok huik – Jon thomstone – Jok bell his sundis – Jhonn armestrang of calsteild – Jhonn Rowclege – Daud armestrang – James roger will michel – sone Thomas aikinheid – Jon huik – niniane armstrang of there neif – christie armstrang his sone Jhonn litill – Jhonn croffet – Jon armestrang in hoilhous – Jon armestrang in glinzer – andro armstrang – his son rowe wm and christie armstrangeris breth to the said Jon – will armstrang in teikmie – Thome armstrang in glinzer – geordie armstrang in blakbakheid – Johnn Irving in sikheid – geordie Jon and christie Irvingis sonis to gib in blakbakfyd John Irving in hag – Jok moffat in glinzer – armstrang in thornyquhattie – Jhonn turner thair – niniane rurnor thair – archie archie armestrang in tarkima archie and ror armestrangis sonis to cristie in langholme – Iyngrie armestrang of raltoun – richie Irving in Auchinruvok – Sandie Irving thair – Jon carruthers in glinzer – cristie michelsone in tuimschelburne – John Michelsone his sone thair – will coltert and thome wilsone thair – andrew turner thair – archie armestrange nicheand – William armestrang callit kynmont – Jon geordie thome sandie Jhonn and Ringane armstrangis Sonis to Kynmont – ror grahme duelland on Serk watter – Wm Scott and Thomas reidpeth – Jon lintoun and willie bell thair – geordie litill thair – mertine thomsone thair – Dave baty thair – Jame cowane thair – andro giffert and Ror makilwitty writter to kinmont – archie and adame thomsonis – nicoll baty in carlisgill – will litill – als pyk ekie – Dick and wat litillis – niniane thome george and will ellatis – Jon armestrang in Wauchoipdaill – henrie ade archie Jon and Syme litillis – Jon armestrang als reltoun will sandie and Jok armestrangis – george baty in nedder croisdykis – Niniane palmer – Jon purdoun – Jame irving – Dandy andro and cristie armestrang in capilgill – Jynkin grahme in logane – pet grahame and pait bell thair – mathow Irving – matho baty – Jon lind – say mrk – alexr and thome carrtheris – Jok and archie batyis – Geordie thomsone in kirkgill – Joke thomesone and adie and Joke thomsonis – his breter wat in allebaitland – John thomsone thair – John thomson in Kirkgill – archie thomsone in allebasterland – nikie and Jok thomsonis thair – Jon thomsone in pollorane – Hector armestrang in stubholme – geordie armestrang in arkiltoun Niniane geordie ni tine Dandy and mingo armestrangis his sonis Niniane and hobie armestrangis – andro litill – Willie broun – Willie nielsone – edut littill – Jon armestrang – Rakaf – Willie grahme – thome Scott in Blakhall – Jon scot his sone – Jon ellot in wod end – rowe ello of there – hall hob and will ellottis bres. – Riche grahme in wodend – willie ellat – lord archie armstrang in arkiltoun – Jon armestrang his sone – adam scott in mospebill – Jhonn scott his sone Jon geordie and will Scottis – Jok scott in arkiltoun – archie Irving thair – Jok ellat in bowgranis – Ninian armestrang thair – lairdis Niniane Joke armstrang his sone – Johnn armestrang howgill – Andro armestrang – thome kirkpatrik – andro turnor – Jhonn armestrang in muklehirst – Jon niniane and christie armstrangis brethers – rowe armestrang – the lairdis rowe Jon and ringane armettragis his sons – Jenkin archie and willie nielson – tom litill – tom armestrang of gryneuk – abe ringine – christie archie thome Jok and ade armestrangis his sonis – wattie mathew george Sim and jon litillis – ade glendonig – Thom coltert – ade hoip – Rowe armestrang of brumholme – Thome armestrang sone to the lairdis rowe geordie thomesoun – george armstrang in catgill – wm wilsoun – Jon moffet – ade and Jon batyis – Jon purwes – James waugh – Ringane armestrang of auchinbedrig – Sim thomas and ror armetrangis – James and alexr halydays – christie Jon – arthour and thome bellis – andro lowrie – arche lawart – adame pott – George armestrang in betholme – patone armestrang thair – rob halyday – andro baty – Jon grahme in hoilll – Dauid and archie grahmes – Symon grahme in logane – george robe and Jok batyis – Mertein Moffet – Jok and thome wilsonis – serge halyday – umphra rewll – Jon Irving – Thome hendersone in brekanquhat –

Wmphra bell alias lamb – Jon corrie – Jhonne kirkpatrk – Willie millair – serge armestrang brother to kynmont – Jon Johonestoun – Jeffra Irving – archie Irving – Jok grahme – Rob clerk – willie kirkpatrik – Dauid watsone – wattie grahme – thomas Jhonnstoune – adame george and richie raes – Christie armestrang in carron – Quhintting andro and geordie armestrangeis – brether cristie armestrang – sone to quitine – Jok armestrang sone to andro – Niniane armestrang sone to patonis niniane geordie armestrang in thornyquhatt – cristie armestrang callit armestrangis cristie – Jon turnor in torniquhatt – Jame armestrang in carrono – Thome armestrang of gyngillis sone to andro – ade murray – willie dryane – Jame and archie litillis – archie baty – mathe litill – Jame litill – edut ringane and lance armestrangis – willie scott – ade scott – ale archie and georde armestrangis – ade and Jame grahmes – rogr. armestrang – Ikie armestrang gyngill – andro armestrange – his son thome armestrang – hob and alie wilsonis – geordie armestrang – nekie grahme – Jynkin Dauie gibbie – Jon Jok bartie and sandie litillis – peter Jok and alexr bellis – cudde litill – Joke irving – andro bell – Jame bell – alexr armestrang of the gingill – Thome armestrang in craig sone to alexr – mathow litill thair – arche willie and hewe armestrangis the gynglier – Sim litill laird of mekill Daill – archie wattie John and adie litillis – Jon scott – andro litill – Jok turnor in kirk toun – Cudde litill thair – Jon scot thair – willie stevinsone thair – George armestrang howgill – andro henderson thair – thome armestrang of the wray – Jok armestrang – will litill in bombie – geordie and Jon litles brer – Jesper geordie will rob nekie and Jok litillis thair Jok litil sone to Jhonn litill – Wattie litill and Niniane armestrang in brumholme – Jon ekie and antonie armestrangis

8

‌—ᙦ ᙣ—

Ewes War Memorial

Inscription at top

IN HONOUR OF THE MEN OF THIS PARISH WHO GAVE
THEIR LIVES FOR THEIR COUNTRY IN THE GREAT WAR
1914–1918

Sergt. John Forrester, M.M.	K.O.S.B.
Pte. Harry Armstrong	Gordons
Pte. David Blacklock	K.O.S.B.
Pte. William Boyes	K.O.S.B.
Pte. John Davidson	K.O.S.B.
Pte. Thomas Hogg	K.O.S.B.
Pte. Thomas Irving	K.O.S.B.
Pte. John Musgrave	K.O.S.B.
Corpl. Robert Rigg	Gordons
Pte. William Campbell	Gordons
Pte. David Campbell	H.L.I.
Pte. William Sinclair	Black Watch
Pte. George Scott	Black Watch

Inscription at foot of Memorial

WE HAIL THE GLORY DAWNING IN IMMANUELS LAND

Ewes Church today, looking from the main entrance off the A7 road

9

_⊙⁓⊙_

Additional Notes

MR ROBERT DARLING – Said to have been the only Episcopal Minister who served the Parish of Ewes but of this there is some doubt since, between the suspension of John Lithgow in 1664 and the Revolution in 1688, two Ministers are named as holding the living and in 1694 when Darling was presented, the Presbyterian form of worship had been restored

The efforts of Charles II to destroy the Presbyterian form of church government in Scotland and introduce Episcopacy, met with unbending resistance from people in Scotland, especially from those of the lowland counties. The policy of the King found fitting expression in the decree of the Council of Glasgow – "the drunken Council" – in 1662, known as the Collation Act, which required every Presbyterian minister who had been ordained since 1649, as a condition of retaining his incumbency, to obtain nomination thereto, and to submit to re-ordination by a bishop.

JOHN LITHGOW – The Minister of Ewes at the date of the decree, he was ordained to the pastoral charge in 1646 and was therefore not required to undergo re-ordination to retain his living.

He persistently refused to conform and in 1664 was suspended.

He retired to a property he owned at Reidpath on the Tweed where he met, and was intimate terms with, Henry Erskine, father of Ebenezer and Ralph Erskine, the founders of the Secession Church.

He became involved in preaching at conventicles, or field-preaching until he was apprehended in 1682 and taken to Edinburgh for trial.

On being charged, he refused to take the oath and was condemned to imprisonment on the Bass Rock. However, on petition, he was permitted the alternative or "removing furth of the Kingdom". Eventually, in 1688, John Lithgow was restored to the kirk of Ewes where he continued his ministry until 1694, when he finally retired to Reidpath.

REV. ROBERT MALCOLM of Lochore, Fife was presented to the living of Nether-Ewes with Over-Ewes, by the Earl of Dalkeith who also gave him the tenancy of a sheep-farm on the Esk at Burnfoot, at a nominal rent to assist the small stipend at Ewes.

GEORGE MALCOLM, son of Robert Malcolm, known as of Douglen, married Margaret Pasley of Craig, and managed the farm.

Four of their sons received knighthoods, referred to locally as the "Four Knights of Eskdale".

SIR JAMES MALCOLM entered Royal Marines and served some forty-eight years. A friend of Lord Nelson, he saw active service first in Spain and later in America in 1812, and was awarded the G.C.B for his services.

SIR PULTENEY MALCOLM entered the navy at an early age under his uncle Admiral Sir Thomas Pasley. After a long and distinguished naval career he became a Rear-Admiral in 1813.

In 1815 he co-operated with Lord Wellington in the Peninsular Campaign and he commanded the St Helena station (1816–1817) while Napoleon was in captivity. He was Commander-in-Chief Mediterranean 1828–1831 and again 1833–1834. A statue in his honour was erected in St. Paul's Cathedral.

SIR JOHN MALCOLM entered the services of the East India Co., the age of 13 years. He was a cadet in Madras and saw active service against Tippoo Tib. In 1798 was appointed by Lord Wellesly assistant to the Resident of Hyderabad. He became the Ambassador to Persia and given the rank of Major General. He was knighted in 1815. After his death in 1833 a statue in his honour was erected in Westminster Abbey.

SIR CHARLES MALCOLM entered Naval Services at the age of 15 years and served in the East Indies 1797–1803. During the Napoleonic War he served in the North Sea, off the coasts of France and Portugal and in the West Indies. He was invalided from West Indies in 1819, and from 1822 to 1827 was stationed in Ireland. He received his knighthood from Lord Wellesly, Lord Lieut. of Ireland. He was made Rear Admiral in 1837 and became Admiral in 1847.

REV. RICHARD SCOTT presented by Henry, Duke of Buccleuch 17th September 1761, He died 13th February 1790 in his 62nd year of age and 31st in the ministry. He was described as "fervant in the divine service, steady and loyal in friendship and mild and gentle in manner, his life exhibited a pattern to his flock". He married 24th April 1761, Mary Turnbull and had five sons, of whom James was a merchant in New York, and John and George merchants in London, and three daughters.

REV. JOHN CLUNIE was Precentor at Markinch, presented by Henry, Duke of Buccleuch and ordained 28th September 1790. He transferred to Borthwick 12th April 1791.

REV. JOHN LAURIE transferred from Eskdalemuir, presented by Henry, Duke of Buccleuch and admitted 29th September 1791. He died 5th April 1817 aged 72 and in his 32nd year in the ministry. He married Anne Grieve and had six sons, three of whom achieved rank in the Royal Marines, and two daughters.

REV. ROBERT SHAW – Minister, writer of the article for the "Statistical Account" of 1841. His brother Rev. William B. Shaw was Minister in Langholm. The brothers were Ministers of the adjoining parishes for a continuous period of thirty-six years.

Mr Malcolm's induction to the Parish of Ewes is recorded thus: it is the first entry in the old surviving Ewes Parish Minute Book.

THE RECORDS OF THE ACTS AND PROCEEDINGS OF THE SESSION OF EWIS
BEGINNING UPON THE 21ST DAY OF MARCH 1717 YEARS

Ewis church March 21, 1717

The Heretors and Elders of this parish haveing made application to the Presbytry of Midlebie to appoint one of their number to moderate a call to Mr. Robert Malcolm Preacher of the Gospel to be Minister in this place, the Presbytery appointed for that effect Mr. John Mein, who, after performing divine service this day in the congregation, did constitute by prayer the meetting of Heretors, Elders and Heads of familys, and Arthur Armstrong the Clerk calling the Roll of their names, they voted for Mr. Malcolm, subscribed a Call to him and nominated Arkletoun and Arthur Henderson their Commissioners to present the said call to the Presbytery to meett att Killpatrick on the 27th instant and to prosecute the same. The Moderator concluded with prayer. He attested the call in the following manner

> "I Mr. John Mein Minister of the Gospel at Westerkirk doe attest that conforme to the Presbytry of Midlebee's appointment I did moderate att the meetting of the Electors in the parish of Ewis. And all the Heretors and Elders and all the Masters of familys present did by their vote make choice of Mr. Robert Malcolm Probationer to be their Pastor and subscribed the above written call unto him. In witnes whereof I have subscribed these presents att Westerkirk the 25th day of March 1717 year" Sic Subscribitur Jo: Mein

Ewis Church August 19, 1717

Mr. Malcolm was this day ordained by the Reverend Presbytry,

Mr. James Curry Minister att Hoddam haveing presided in the ordination and preached upon 1 Thess. 5.ch.12, 13 And we beseech you brethren to know them which labour among you, and are over you in the Lord, and admonish you, and to esteem them verry highly in love for there works sake

10

Militia List

T HE list of names given here, was taken from a manuscript note-book, discovered in a small museum, in Langholm Town Hall. This note-book contains a list of all the men in the Eskdale Parishes, who were eligible for service in the militia, which was raised in the year 1802, in the face of a threat of invasion by the Emperor Napoleon.

The list is of particular value and interest since it gives, not only the names of the men, but also their occupation and the names of their dwelling places.

A summary of the contents of the note-book, which is entitled "Lieutenancy Minutes for Subdivision of Eskdale", has appeared in the Transactions of the Dumfriesshire and Galloway Antiquarian Society, published 1969.

(There is no longer a museum in Langholm Town Hall.)

AMOS	William	Carrotrigg	Farmer
ANDERSON	George	Bush	Servant
ANDERSON	James	Blackhall	Servant
ANDISON	Christopher	Burngrains	Shepherd
ANDISON	James	Fiddletonbank	Roadmaker
ANDISON	Michael	Fiddletonbank	Roadmaker
ARMSTRONG	John	Wrae	—
BEATTIE	Charles	Unthank	Servant
BORTHWICK	Alexander Hay	Sorbie	Tenant
BORTHWICK	Walter	Muckledale	—

CLEGHORN	John	Flaskholmhead	Shepherd
DAVIDSON	William	Westside	Shepherd
DICKSON	Francis	Brierishaw	Shepherd
DOUGLAS	James	Burnfoot	Servant
DRYDON	Thomas	Carrotrigg	Servant
EASTON	Robert	Howgill	Shepherd
ELLIOT	John	Middlemass	Shepherd
ELLIOT	Robert	Howgill	Weaver
FULTON	Alexander	Brierishaw	Servant
GRAY	William	Bush	Servant
GRIEVE	John	Howgill	Weaver
GRIEVE	Thomas	Bush	Shepherd
HALL	James	Fiddletonbank	Labourer
HALLIDAY	James	Nether Fedling	Labourer
HOGG	Richard	Nether Fedling	Servant
HOGG	Thomas	Blackhall	Servant
HYSLOP	Walter	Cooms	Shepherd
IRVING	Archibald	Burnfoot	Servant
IRVING	John (Jr.)	Glendevan	—
IRVING	William	Glendevan	—
JACKSON	James	Arkleton	Servant
JACKSON	James	Arkleton	Shepherd
JACKSON	John (Jr.)	Sandyhaugh	—
JARDINE	John	Arkleton	—
JOHNSTON	Thomas	Fiddletonbank	Labourer
KEIN	James	Fiddletonbar	Tollgatherer
LITTLE	Archibald	Terrona	Tenant
LITTLE	Matthew	Mosspeeble	Shepherd
LITTLE	Ninian	Burnfoot	Tenant
LITTLE	Simon	Burnfoot	—
LITTLE	William	Unthank	Servant
LOCKIE	John	Sorbie	Servant
LUNN	Robert	Ewislees	Servant
LITTLE	Walter	Terrona	Tenant
MITCHEL	James	Glendevan	Servant
MOFFAT	William	Mosspeeble	Tenant
MOORE	John	Muckledalehaugh	Ploughman

MURRAY	George	Lodgegill	Shepherd
MURRAY	John	Sorbie	Shepherd
MURRAY	John	Ewis (sic) Manse	Servant
MURRAY	Matthew	Howgill	Weaver
MURRAY	Simon	Carrotrigg	—
MURRAY	Thomas	Carrotrigg	—
NICHOL	Archibald	Flaskholmhead	Labourer
PARK	William	Carrotrigg	Shepherd
PEARSON	William	Burnfoot	Mole Catcher
REID	Peter	Ewislees	Servant
RIDDELL	William	Mosspeeble	Tenant
ROOKE	William	Bush	Mole Catcher
SCOTT	Andrew	Mosspeeble	Tenant
SCOTT	Archibald	Kirkstyle	Mason
SCOTT	George	Lodgegill	Shepherd
SCOTT	John	Muckledale	Shepherd
SCOTT	Robert	Carrotrigg	Farmer
SCOTT	William	Ewislees	Servant
STORY	William	Wrae	Servant
TELFER	Richard	Fiddletonbank	Roadmaker
THOMSON	Andrew	Carrotrigg	Servant
THOMSON	James	Bankend	Shepherd
TURNBULL	James	Brierrishaw	Servant
TURNBULL	William	Burnfoot	Servant
WELSH	William	Kirktonburnside	Weaver

Meikledale in Ewes Valley

11

~∽◞∾~

Session Minutes

Extracts of Ewes Session Minutes :

Ewes Church, the thirteenth day of October 1867.

The Kirk Session met and was constituted by prayer. Rev. Thomas Smith, Moderator Messrs Dryden, Little, Lyall and Welsh, Elders. Resolved

To record that the new Parish Church was this day opened for public worship, when the Rev. Mr Smith, Minister of the Parish, read and expounded 1 Kings 8.12–30 and Luke 8.9–14, and the Rev. Dr Monro of Campsie preached an able, eloquent and appropriate sermon from Proverbs 11.30 "He that winneth souls is wise".

To express the Kirk Session's gratitude for the beautiful and elegant Church and their satisfaction with the comfort convenience and accommodation therein provided.

To record the Kirk Session's thanks to those parishioners and others who have voluntarily contributed towards the expense of the stained-glass windows put into the new House of God; and to the Rev. Archibald Malcolm, Vicar of Dunsten, Oxfordshire and great-grandson of the Rev. Robert Malcolm, once minister of this parish for his presentation of a new handsomely bound Bible for the services of the Church.

The Kirk Session instructed the Clerk to copy into their Minute Book the allocation made of the pews in the Church and to note the former and present positions of the tombstones belonging to Mr. Scott Elliot of Arkleton.

Allocation of seats in the new Church of Ewes

Pew No 1 & 2	Terrona & Wrae
3	Terrona
4. 5. 6.	Arkleton
7	Duke of Buccleuch (Potholm)
8	Potholm servants
9	Burnfoot
10	Bunfoot & Fiddleton Tollbars
11 & 12	Sorbie
13 & 14	Mosspeeble
15 & 16	Unthank
17	Eweslees & Fiddleton
18	Eweslees
19	Glendiven
20	Blackhall
21	Brieryshaw (Joiner)
22	Church Officer
23	Minister
24	Schoolmaster
25	Carrotrigg
26. 27. 28. 29	Meikeledale
30	Cooms
31	Brieryshaw (Blacksmith)
32	Cooms
33	Kirkstyle
34	Brieryshaw
35	Howgill
36	Howgill & Flaskholm
37 & 38	Bush

Of the tombstones referred to in the foregoing Minute the larger one which has been placed at the passage in the north end of the new Church was formerly against the north wall of the old Church exactly facing the west door the smaller one which has been placed in the east wall beside pew No. 6 in the new Church stood formerly below the stair in the south west corner of the old Church

October 24 1867   The Kirk Session agreed to pay Jane Welsh one shilling a week for cleaning the Church from this date, and to raise the salary of the Officer to two pounds in respect of his having now to take charge of the heating apparatus.

Other Extracts:

Sept. 10, 1717   The Minister desired the Elders to informe him what utensils belonged to the Church and off the state of the poors money. They told him.

That for the Communion service they had a silver cup which was at present in Arkletouns custody, fowr long tables, eight furms and also tickets and two long table cloaths, which William Murray produced, And that they had timber for a tent.

That there was a peuther bason for baptism. That for digging of graves and funeralls there was a spade, a shovell and how. And a mortcloath with a wallet which Arthur Henderson produc'd.

That there was a ladder for repairing the Kirk. That there was one Register from 1694 to 1701 and the minuts of the Session not yet recorded from the 30th of March 1701 to the 21st of March last which William Murray produced

May 17, 1718   The Schoolmaster being returned from the University which he had attended by the Sessions permission, the School now again committed to his care and he was desired to give in att the next Sederunt a list of the poor Scholars. No complaint was made of Thomas Moffets managing the school dureing the Masters absence

Sept. 6, 1719   The Session takeing to consideration a list laid before them of these persons who have been Ministers since the Reformation in this parish till the year 1717 And finding it improper to suffer their memorys to perish and that some of them would have been forgotten had it not been for one or two aged people, they did and hereby doe appoint them to be recorded as followeth Messrs William Graham, Robert Chisholm, John Linlithgow, John Hume, John Melvill and Robert Darling. The two first died Ministers here; the 3rd served ye cure from 1646 to 1664 and from the late Revolution till about ye time his assistant was ordain'd and that ye consummatness of his age inclin'd him to leave ye place; the 4th went out because of ye test; the 5th continued till the Revolution and ye 6th from ye 1694 to ye 1716 when he died.

Dec. 1, 1718   There haveing been no stair for some time bygone to ascend by to the pulpit, only loose stonns and turf, the Session resolved to have a timber stair and recommended to the Minister to order the makeing thereof and to report when it is done, the Session is to pay it till the money be recovered off the Heretors.

Dec. 12, 1721   After prayer Sederunt Mr Malcolm Minister, Edward Atchison Elder and William Young and Robert Niccol deacons. Arkletoun in dead. Matthew Murray absent. Edward Atchison's excuse for his absence from some former Sederunts was sustain'd.

May 20, 1722   The Minister represented that Matthew Murray in Wrea and John Clement his herd boy having lately on a Lords day been scolding and fighting he had called for John who was obliged to goe off from the place before the Session could meett and rebuked him for breach of Sabbath and taken his promise to doe no more so And had sent word to Matthew to wait this day on the Session, Matthew being allowed to come in confessed the crime, professed his sorrow for it, promised amendment and was rebuked.

March 3 post meridiem (1723)   It being represented that ane John Rae in the parish of Eskdalemoor had been for some time at Meikledale and yoaked, to the offence of the Congregation, his Carr on the Lords day to carry fodder to his cattle and the said

John was now gone back to Eskdalemoor. The Session recommended to the Minister to desire Mr Lowry to admonish the said John Rae for his offensive behaviour in this place.

March 1, 1724   Th: Mitchels collection was deliver'd to his Relict he being dead and And: Lamb haveing represented that she desire to be excus'd from paying for the Mortcloath at her husbands funeral, her desire was granted.

Simeon Little reported that the people are willing to make use of the Mortcloath

Jan. 7, 1728   The Session appoint Mat: Murray to enquire att a wright the lowest price for which he can make coffins for the poor in this parish.

Resolved to order the cutting of the ground where the Lords supper is usually dispensed for the more convenient situation of the tables, in case the tennants of the ground agree to it, and it is recommended to the Minister to speak with them and to see to the execution of this design.

Feb. 4, 1728   The Clerk reports that James Mitchell and his mother are waiting att the door. The Session allowed them to come in, and James haveing read a pairt of the Bible indifferently well, his Mother desired that the Session might allow him another quarter, which was granted unto her.

Mat: Murray reportes that Jo: Johnstone in Langholme is willing to make coffins for the poor att 5.sh:sterline each, which the Session being willing to give, Mat: is to give inforation of the Sessions mind unto Jo: Johnstone.

The Minister reports that the tennants were willing to allow the ground to be cutt for the communion tables, that it was cutt accordingly and that the Treasurers had payed sixteen pence for the doing of it.

May 18, 1729   The Treasurer represented that Mr Woods happence being cryed down att the cross, and publick intimation haveing been made from the pulpit to cast no bad money in to the box, they had sold all their bad happence att a third part loss.

It being represented that since Jo: Scot was dead, his relick Jean Johnston was att liberty to go abroad for Alms, therefore the Session Resolved that she needed no quarterly pension from them, but should be provided with shoes.

Oct. 7, 1731   The Clerk represented that he could not get account of the ages of the dead frequently, therefore it was resolved not to mention the age in the Register of the dead.

Feb. 18, 1733   Resolved that 3 pence be payed for the horse speaks: 2 pence for the hand speaks and that the coarse hand speaks left att funerals be given gratis.

May 19, 1734   Resolved to buy a plank of wood for a table, a tree to be made into seats and 20 yeards of linnen for the Communion service. For all the Communicants being seated att once, and never raised till the service is over, therefore the old tables, furms and linnen are not sufficient.

Jan. 19, 1735   Resolved that all the money that hath been gott, or shall be gott for private marriages in consequence of the Sessions Act, the 2 of Aug. 1719, is not poors money, but may be applied to publick usees shuch as the building and repairing of styles to the Churchyeard, and the like occasions, if other funds fail that may be laid on for these ends.

March 27, 1735   It was represented that the parochiners had made a cast of £3 for the style and necessaries for the Sacrament. The Treasurers represented that the collection made for Js. Young the poor widdow in Terrona that had been made in the church lately with the consent of the parochiners and the members of the Session was delivered unto her.

Oct. 19, 1735   Resolved that the Minister shal collect the mony cast in for the stile and the Comunion Linin, but that in the meantime the style and the linin be payd by the Treasarours, out of the Penalty Mony.

Hugh Scott hath ben rebuked for the seccond time; and it was resolved to rebuike him no more till his prior guilt in Casteltoun is purged.

Resolved that a new long ladder be got, and that the old ladder be cut into a short one.

The Ballance of the Tresarours Acompts on the end of June last was £3/19/9d It being credibly reported, that the mony owing to the Session by John Chisholm was in danger, an order of arestment was gott, and laid upon mony due to John by Mathew Murray, Mathew has given his bill for £6/12/od Scots which pays all Johns principal and intrest, excep 9 Shilings, for which he has given his bill, and hath got up his bond of a discharge of the debt all which the Session approved of.

It being represented that Wm. Renick in Sorbie had beat last Lords day Robt. Lamb in Kirktown, and that he was waiting at the door to acknowledge his breach of Sabbath: he was allowed to come in and having confesed his fault was rebuked for it.

Feb. 15, 1736   The ladders are ordered according to appointment. The Treasarours represented that John Scott Tenant in Cronksbank had mortified £4 'S' to the poor of this Parish, that it was payd in by Thomas Scott his son, that it was discharged by the Minister in name of the Session. That Mrs. Atchison, Ewis Lees had also payd £5 'S' mortified to the poor by Robt. Atchison Tenant in Ewis Lees her husband, and that the Minister had also given her a Discharge for the mony. This the Session approved of.

It being represented that the Elders could not see to read in the Elders seat, a window is to be broken out for it and to be payd out of the Penalty and Marriage Mony.

Isobel Irvin a poor woman in Kirktoun is admitted a Pantioner at £0/2/6 a quarter, and £0/9/2 were ordred, to buy half a Boal of Meal, for Robt. Andisons poor family in Kerriot-ridg, and the Treserors were ordered to pay the coffens for Robt. Laidlaw in Buss and Jean Bell in Burnfoot.

It being represented that John Stodhert and Isobel Hall were scandalously reported of, by John Elliot their neighbor. The Minister, Arkeltoun and Mathew Murray were apointed as a Comitie to ripen this afair for the next Session.

Resolved to appoint to every elder several Quarters of the Parish (viz) To Robt. Laidlaw Kerriot Rig, Burnfoot, Blackhall, Ewislees and Unthank. To Wm. Lamb, Mospeeble, Mukledeal and Burngrange. To Arkeltoun, Buss and Arkeltoun. To Wm. Young, Glendiven and Tarras. To Andrew Lamb, Breary Shaw, Kirkstile and Kirktoun. To Adam Drydon, Sorby and Hoghill and to Mathew Murray, Flask, Wrea and Terona.

The Session find that 3 Sh to Marry Elliott, 2 Sh to Jean Jonston, 2 Sh 6d to Isobel Irvin, 2 Sh 6d to Wm. Hyslop, and 5 Sh to Jenet Elliott, ordinary Quarterly pentioners, amounts to 15 Sh in the Quarter, which is £3/0/0 by year. And that £1 pound is given yearly to other poor paritioners who are not ordinary Quarterly pentioners. That 5 Sh yearly is given to strangers having Testimonials. And that £1/12 Sh/0 is given yearly to the Session, Presbytry, Synods Clerks and Oficers in all £5/7/0 expended yearly by the Session, besides quartr wages for the poor Scholars.

Aug. 5, 1736 The poor Scholars are allowd to continue at School, and the Minister is to try their proficiency.

The window in the Elders seat is made according to appointment The mony appointed to be given out the last Sederunt was given according to appointment.

The Comitie report that they had conversed with John Stodhert and Isobel Hall, as also with John Elliott: and that upon full inquiry into the afair their appeared neither proof of guilt nor foundation for a proces. Therefore it is recomended to the Minister to Intimat this from the pulpit, in order to repair the good name of the parties concernd, and that people may think charitably of those against whom no proof of guilt hath appeared.

Mathew Murrah represented that since new linnin was provided for the comunion service, he had with the advice of the other Elders, sold the remains of the old worne linnen for 2 Sh. This was approvd of.

Jan. 9, 1737 The Tresaurours represented that Thomas Murray in
the Parish of Langholm, had given to them a Bill for £20/0/0 Scots,
as a leagacie to the poor of this parish from Mathew Murray his
deceesd Brother.

The Session recomended to the Minister to order a Broad to be
made for the Inscription of this legacy and of Jo. Scots legacy
mentioned in the Sederunt of the 15ᵗʰ Feby. 1736.

May 15, 1737 Answer is returnd to the Sessions letters as followeth
viz. A letter from Arkeltoun excusing himself from finding conjunct
security for his debt to the Session, because it was not Borrowed
mony, but the Gratuity of his mother and Grandfather; and another
letter from Wm. Little in Kirkstile promising payment of his
principal sume at Lambas next, and theirfor excusing himself from
further conjunct security till that time.

The Session sustaind those excuses and appointed Arkeltoun to
aquaint James Paislay, that now Mr. Hanchalwood was dead, who
had been conjunctly bound with him to the Session, he behouved
to find another to bind conjunctly with him for the Debt.

July 24 1737 The minister represented that he had, with the consent
and advice of the members of the Session and of the Presbytry,
laid before the Commisioners of his grace the Duik of Buckclough
a petition showing that his Session cannot find good security for
the poors mony, that theirfor they inclind to apply pairt of it for
the building of an Alms House for the use of the poor of the parish,
but that their being no ground to be had except what belongd to
his Grace, Glendivvan would be the most convenient situation,
and that the Tennant consented unto it and theirfor praying that
liberty might be granted for building in that place, as also the
privaledge of Divots fairns for that thing and the use of the Peat
moss to the poor inhabitants. He represented also that the said
Commisioners had granted the Petition upon condition that a
suficancy of moss was found both for the Tennants and also for
the poor; and he laid before the Session as estimate for an house
to accomadate eight inhabitants amounting to £14/7s/6d. all which

the Session approved of but delay the farther consideration of the said Alms Hous till Mr. Scott the Chamberlin inquire into the state of the Moss.

The Confession of Faith

We the Minister Elders and Schoolmaster in the parish of Ewis haveing considered the Acts of the Generall assembly dated at Edinburgh on the 16th and 17th days of Feberruary 1700 appointing all Ministers Ruling Elders and School-masters to subscribe the Confession of faith, as the confession of their faith according to the formula agreed upon in the isth Act of Assembly 1694. Do sincerely own and declare the above confession of faith, approven by former Generall Assamblys of this church and Ratifyd by law in the year 1690 to be the confession of our faith, and that we own the doctrine therein contained, to be the true Doctrine, which we will constantly adhere to, as likeways that we own and acknowledge presbyterian Church Government of this Church, now setled by law, by Kirk Session, presbyteries, provintiall Synods and Generall Assemblys, to be the only Government of this Church, And that we will submitt thereto concur therewith, And never endeavour directly or indirectly the prejudice or subversion thereof, And that we shall observe uniformity of Worship, And of the administration of all publick Ordinances within this church as the same are at present perfoormed and allowed. In testimony whereof we have subscribed in Ewis Church.

Upon the 24th day of November one thousand seven hundred and twenty years Robert Malcolm minister

Wm Elliot Elder

William Murray Elder

Arthur Armstrong Schoolmaster

Subscribed in Ewis church upon the 5th day of August one thousand seven hundred and twenty two years by Junon ? Elder Matthew Murray Elder & William Young

March 1 1724 subscribed by William Angus Schoolmaster

March 29, 1730 Subscribed by Archibald Johnson

Octr 2, 1746 Subscribed by Thos Scott Elder

Robert Laidla Eldes.

Andrew Lamb Elder

Will Caston Elder & Schoolmaster

July 19th 1747 Subscribed by John Turnbull Schoolmaster

June 5th 1757 Subscribed by Robert Hotson Elder

John Elliot Elder

Feb ? by Subscribed James Laidlan Elder

Novr 17 1805 by John Little Elder

William Murray Elder John Armstrong Elders

John Lohy Elder

The page in the Session Minute Book which the Elders signed

Extracted from the Valuation Roll of the County of Dumfries
(Printed 1827)

ANCIENT VALUATION (1671)

Parish of Ewes	Mks.	s.	d.
The Duke of Buccleugh's valuation in this parish, Stock and Teind, with feu maills, extends to	6325	0	0
The lands of Arkletoune, pertaining to Walter Elliot	700	0	0
The lands of Meikledale, pertaining to Adam Elliot	900	0	0
The Six-merkland of Sorbie	250	0	0
The land of Tarras	1100	0	0
The lands of Brieryshaw	90	0	0
SUMA	9365	0	0

Nyne thousand three hundreth sixty-fyve merks.

MODERN VALUATION (1823)

Duke of Buccleuch and Queensberry	Lodgegill, or Black Tarras	550	0	0
	Six-merkland of Sorbie	250	0	0
	Brieryshaw	90	0	0
	His Grace's whole other lands in this parish	6325	0	0
		7215	0	0
Thomas Beattie of Crieve	Meikledale	900	0	0
William Elliot of Arkleton	Arkleton, part of Tarras	700	0	0
James Elliot of Cooms	Cooms, part of Tarras	550	0	0
		9365	0	0

Total Valuation of the parish of Ewes,
Nine thousand three hundred and sixty-five merks.

Minister's stipend, 15 chalders, half meal, half barley, and £8 6s 8d for Communion elements. Last augmentation dated 18th Dec. 1822. School salary, 400 merks.